40

YEARS
AN INNKEEPER

History, Stories, and Recipes from Napa Valley's Famed
WINE COUNTRY INN
Rated One of the Top Small Hotels in the United States

JIM SMITH

40 Years an Innkeeper

Contents

CHAPTER 1
The Cast

My father, Ned Smith, the creator of The Wine Country Inn, located in the heart of the Napa Valley, was a great and frightened man. He was larger than life when out in public, but I'm sure when the lights came down, his dark demons came to visit. There are a million stories I could tell to illustrate my perceptions of him and maybe as this piece moves along I will get into some of those, but this is supposed to be a story about The Wine Country Inn and life in the Napa Valley so I will try to stay on task.

Before we moved to the Napa Valley Ned had been an Ad Man in San Francisco. He worked for what I guess you

Ned Smith

would call an advertising broker by the name of Blair TV. The way he explained it to us kids, TV and radio stations would assign advertising time slots on their channels to the Ad Men who were in charge of selling these slots to advertisers. My father headed up the TV division of the company and my uncle Heb ran the radio end. Visions of the television show "Mad Men" come to mind every time I think of those stories.

As a child, I understood that my dad would slog from our home in Orinda (a bedroom community of San Francisco) every morning to meet clients. He would glad-hand them a little at his office, talk about family and how the guy's travels went, engage in small talk and then head off for the "men's club." There, they would play a little squash or handball, hit the steam room and maybe get a little rub-down. (I always imagined Brunhilda pounding them with massive arms and the weight to back them up, but now, as an adult, I am imagining maybe something a little different). Then came lunch and the mandatory two or three martinis. According to my dad, they would

then navigate back to his office to talk actual business and sign contracts. Now that I think about it, and after watching every episode of Mad Men, I can no longer imagine my father's office without a couch. Now that I'm 61, I can't envision that lifestyle without an afternoon nap, for according to my father in those days it was terribly impolite to leave a travelling businessman alone in a strange city at night. So, of course, the party would continue. Sometime in the early evening my father would pick up his client for more drinks, a bloody steak and probably some flaming desert (popular in those days) before he would navigate the 20 or so miles home, well after his wife and family were asleep.

At the age of 40 in 1960 my father announced to his wife, Marge, and his kids — three boys and a girl — that the advertising business was a young man's game and that he would be studying for his real estate license. Mad Men has now added so many layers and questions to that remembered announcement. It seemed so simple at the time, but now the nuances and possible alternative explanations swirl in my head. Maybe it is just me projecting my own lovatic sexuality I felt in my 30s, but to think of a man who was completely addicted to money, with four kids and a very nice home giving up a $60,000-a-year job, with stock bonuses every Christmas, in exchange for the uncertainty of real estate sales, I just can't imagine this decision was that simple. I've done the math, and in today's dollars he was bringing in upwards of $400,000–$500,000 a year including the stock he received.

In the summer of 1964 my father uprooted us from suburbia and we were soon living up the long and winding Spring Mountain Road in this Podunk town called St. Helena. Ripped from our friends and our lucrative paper routes, we had landed in the two-bedroom apartment of an abandoned three-story stone castle known as Chateau Chevalier Winery. There was no doubt the building was cool but there were seven of us, following the birth of my younger brother, Jeff. Although this magnificent stone edifice was huge, the livable portion of it was tiny. I'm pretty sure it only had one bathroom, one bedroom for my folks and one bedroom for infant Jeff and younger sister Kate. The three boys slept in the production area of the former winery.

Chateau Chevalier Winery

"It's an adventure," were my father's three most uttered words in those days, seemingly able to justify whatever complaints or complications we might come up with. Like the morning we walked out the front door to find a rattlesnake sunning itself on the stoop, nearly under my mother's foot before she noticed; or the rattlesnake we ran over coming up the long driveway; or the rattlesnakes that lived in large numbers in the blackberry patch just up the hill where the winery's vineyards had been 35 years earlier (the winery had been derelict since Prohibition).

It was certainly an adventure when, after setting up a ping pong table on the second floor of this expansive production room, the bats that lived in the turrets above the third floor would swoop down to investigate the ball in mid-flight. We became well practiced at playing full-on slam games of ping pong while the bats would take turns diving to within millimeters of the ball, yet never touching it and at the same time managing to dodge the paddles we would swing at them from every angle.

And it was certainly an adventure when we modified and commandeered our sister's tricycle (overruling her adamant complaints), set up an obstacle course throughout the winery and eventually ripped the thing apart by pushing it from behind at break-neck speeds, leaning into the turns in a crouch that forced the little wheels sideways until they finally buckled from the force.

One of my most vivid memories was attacking that blackberry patch. For those who have never picked blackberries the first thing you need to know is that blackberries are protected by a thousand tiny thorns per berry (not to mention the rattlesnakes that lurk just a few feet into the thicket). My father was determined to harvest the berries, but he wasn't dumb. Mr. Gott, the caretaker for the property, lived just up the road and he had a jeep. So once we had picked all the berries we could reach without venturing too deeply into the unknown we got in the back of the jeep and my father would back us gently into the thicket that was probably 30 feet in diameter. We picked away, trying to avoid the thorns and eating as many as would land in the bowls we had borrowed from Mom's kitchen until we couldn't reach any more. Then we would all pile out of the jeep, and my father would gently reposition the jeep into virgin bush.

We had a lot of berries by the end of an hour's picking, but Dad knew we would have to give some to the caretaker and probably some to other friends. Besides, these berries were free and enough free stuff was never enough for my father. So, with thousands of berries still so tantalizingly out of reach, before the day was through, my father was backing way up, getting a running start across the uneven hillside and ramming that jeep deep into the bushes, ignoring the tiny specks of blood that he was collecting on his face and arms from the flailing spiky branches.

When the day's picking was done he returned the jeep (apparently no worse for wear) to the caretaker with a couple large bowls of blackberries. Little did we know that the next day we would find THE most amazing gift sitting on the stoop (where the rattlesnake had been a couple weeks earlier) with a note from the caretaker's wife. I have no idea what the note said other than to identify the baker, but 50 years later that Blackberry Refrigerator Pie still stands out as one of my fondest memories of those days. I don't have the original recipe, but I think the following will get you close if you go to the trouble of picking your own berries at the peak of the hot Napa Valley growing season.

My mother was and still is a mysterious woman to me. She turned 90 during the writing of this story while I turned 62. In all those years I don't know that I have ever really got to know her. Even at home my father was always the front man, the entertainer, the disciplinarian, the grand innovator; but my mother was deep, really deep. She was our ally, our arbitrator, but never really our confidant. She played a very fine line between the largeness of our father and the smallness of us kids. But she was always a free-thinker and, man, did she get into trouble here in the conservative Napa Valley in the 60s and 70s.

Deeply opposed to the Vietnam War and always studying international relations, she often turned our dining room table into a battleground with my father and oldest brother against the rest of the family. In outrage my father would actually pound the table; we would absolutely not go to this or that demonstration; we would not go door-to-door campaigning for Eugene McCarthy; we would not continue to produce an underground newspaper. These fights would often follow our folks into the other parts of the house well after dinner was over, but either through continued negotiations or outright defiance my mom and the rest of us would go out anyway to organize or demonstrate.

As an extremely frugal man (I will definitely get into some of these stories later) my father's one big extravagance in moving to the Napa Valley was to join our local Country Club, Meadowood (now a very nice resort). Of course he couldn't allow himself to see it as an extravagance, but rather, as a business necessity, and it probably was. But with my radical and beautiful mother haunting his goldmine it also became the center of great contention. Countless times I

Marge Smith

can remember my parents coming home from one cocktail party or another (many at the Club) with my father livid beyond belief at my mother yet again getting into some political argument with someone. My father, still a newcomer among these second- and third-generation folks, would spend all evening courting the crowd, only to be completely discredited (in his mind) by what I always envisioned as a loud and defiant altercation my mother would get into with one of the other party-goers. Battle lines were really drawn when they started getting dis-invited to the parties and actually excommunicated by my father's closest friend, his brother Heb.

Those were divisive days: drugs, alcohol, the war, dissident newspapers, underground radio stations, social revolutions of a hundred flavors — we had them all here in sunny St. Helena and the Smith family always seemed to be at the center of the trouble. Even the craze of "streaking" (running down Main Street butt-naked as the local movie house is getting out) couldn't be avoided. I'll never forget the late-night call and the explosion of outrage as my father got dressed to go bail my eldest brother out of jail for "indecent exposure." I don't remember my mother ever talking to us all that much about these transgressions, but I know for a fact that she was constantly lobbying in the background or else I'm sure a couple of us would have been shipped off to military school or some such.

Big money was just starting to trickle into the Valley in those days. Prior to that it was all traditional families including the Carpys, the Martinis and the Mondavis (Peter, not Robert). Second- and third-generation landed gentry became close friends of my parents, but I was never sure if that was partly because or partly in spite of my mother. The way I remember it these social gatherings were much more a point of contention between my parents than they were fun evenings. My father insisted on throwing at least four or five dinner parties a year.

It really makes sense to me now that there were so many parties back in those days because outside of peoples' homes there was no decent food in the Valley. It was so bad that every few months my father would cram all seven of us into the car and drive to San Francisco to go out to dinner. Anyway, these dinner parties were tough on my mother. With absolutely no help from my father beyond setting up the bar my mother would be expected to cook, serve and clean-up a lavish dinner for 8 or 12 while juggling five kids and looking fabulous and perspiration-free the whole evening. I truly believe my mother would have been just as happy in a three-room flat in some city, with maybe a kid or two, living a much smaller and more introspective life. Although I never heard her complain (at least not to us kids) I don't remember her expressing great joy either, at least not before we built the Inn.

»————————«

Since I either helped my parents run the Inn or ran it myself for the last 40 years you ought to get to know me a little, too.

In my high school days my father's favorite descriptor for me was "dissolute," and when I complained that I didn't even know what that meant his only comment was "see, if you weren't a dissolute you'd look it up." And he was probably right. This word, which he learned by randomly opening the dictionary every week and picking out a word he was unfamiliar with, certainly didn't apply to my two older brothers. My eldest brother Dave was a staunch "hawk" as we called them in those days, straight A's, pro-Vietnam, student body something — definitely a mover/shaker. My next oldest brother Doug was equally determined, but in exactly the opposite direction; a full-on hippie activist, artist extraordinaire and gleeful corruptor of his younger brother.

And then there was me, the dissolute. I could get decent grades if I applied myself, which I didn't, I had no artistic or athletic skill that I was aware of and my only driving desire in life was to get laid. Sure I was the leader or at least co-leader of my little clique, and I was the younger brother of the notorious troublemaker who got suspended from high school for refusing to say the Pledge Of Allegiance, but I was probably a few inches shorter than most of the girls in my sophomore class and they were all hell-bent on dating the seniors or, as a last resort, the juniors. I was the third-to-smallest kid in my 8th grade graduating class and my first driver's license at 16 described me as 5'3" 113 lbs. Some eighteen months later I had sprouted to 5'11" but still only tipped the scales at about 130. Well into my 30s when I had settled into my final height of 6'2" I was still wearing 28" jeans. I can remember having to buy XL shirts and hand-pleating them in the back every time I would tuck them in to try to keep them from looking like a balloon on me.

It's pretty obvious to me that this is where my real interest in food started. I was eating everything in sight and was still, as a friend's mother called me, Auschwitz-thin. Over the next few years I can remember going out to breakfast at the Yountville Diner (I still miss that place) and eating two complete "workingman's" breakfasts in one sitting and still shaking for more food three hours later. I simply could not eat enough and would devour anything put in front of me. That skinniness, coupled with the fact that I was definitely hanging out with the wrong crowd, left me with no chance in hell with the girls, let alone getting their parents to agree to a date.

With my true ambition effectively blocked, all I could see to do was party and cruise. Main Street St. Helena was not exactly a hopping place back in the late 60's and early 70's (and I'm sure it still isn't for anyone in high school) and I'm not really sure why my parents loaned me the car as much as they did, but I can remember spending endless evenings cruising the strip from the A&W to, say, Morrison's Funeral Home — but wait, I just remembered, I went further than that!

There was this one girl who lived on Main Street, just up from the police station, who seemed to spend as much time on her front porch as I spent in my parents' car. Cute as could be, about my age and completely unknown to me. The house she lived in is still there and about as beat-up as it was back then. But I didn't know her. How could I not have seen this girl at school? There were only 400 kids in total. Even though our love affair went on for easily a couple years we never actually met since the times I would finally ball up

Jim Smith

the courage to stop the car and talk to this beauty her mother would magically appear on the porch. Our faces would fall and I would drive on.

Why is any of this even relevant to this book? What does this have to do with cooking and innkeeping in the present-day Napa Valley? Well, it turns out that being "dissolute," defined as "someone completely lacking in ambition or focus," coupled with my primary goal of getting laid, would play directly into my choice of college.

College? Who the hell said anything about college? I had gotten a good number in the military draft lottery so I didn't have to worry about getting shipped off to Vietnam. I was completely bored in school, pulling decent grades even with my absolute refusal to have anything to do

with homework. Moving out of home right after high school? Who would feed me?

There was this girl. Though I dreamed about her constantly this was not a girl I really had a chance with. She was one of those cheerleader/straight "A" students with a heart of gold and a line of suitors, all of whom she seemed to reject. We definitely had a thing going on, but to my daily disappointment it was almost certainly just a friend thing. She sat behind me in Hampe's class on Communism and she simply would not hear of the idea that I was not going to go to college. During the first semester of our senior year she literally filled out four college applications for me while I stared at her legs and shifted in my seat.

Apparently my grades were good enough to get into my choice of state schools, but when she announced she was going to Chico State I soon followed suit (it was the least I could do to show loyalty to such a staunch friend). Plus, Chico State had been named by Playboy as the best party school in the U.S. for three or four years running. Who knew that the skills I would acquire in college — throwing and hosting parties — would serve me so well in my chosen profession? Plus, of course, my parents informed me that if I didn't go to college I would need to find a job and support myself. That seemed ridiculously old-fashioned and harsh, but they seemed determined to follow through with it, so off to college I went.

Since I refused to live in a dorm I somehow found this tiny room in what I can only now describe as a flop-house, with a shared bathroom, an extremely colorful cast of characters and, if I remember correctly, a communal kitchen that was down one floor and all the way at the other end of the building. I don't really remember much of that first semester other than me slinking to and from classes trying to hide the fact that my boyish good looks had been hijacked by a disfiguring case of cystic-acne that would haunt me for the next twenty years. But there must have been something successful about my experience since, after the second week in Chico, I hitchhiked home to see my family physician who informed me that I would need a couple rounds of penicillin to make things right again.

Colleen was a wreck. She was a sophomore from UC Davis who had apparently come up to Chico for the weekend to get blotto. Her boyfriend had just been shot and killed over the summer by an undercover narc and she was looking for escape, and though I was completely unprepared to help her through her emotional grief I was more than happy to hitchhike down to Davis on a regular basis to give her physical comfort (after she got the penicillin as well).

Vague clouds of memory are floating through my brain now, fleeting images of this guy from Corning who I shared my bathroom with; speed-freaks a floor below me who actually taught me a life-long proverb of their own making (partying and daylight don't mix); and what I now recognize as my first exposure to an aggressively gay kid who convinced me through a couple close calls that I definitely wasn't gay (not that it had ever even occurred to me to wonder).

The flop-house was rough for a kid from St. Helena so after the first semester I started checking the message boards for a roommate situation. I found a house that had four sophomore dudes looking for one more kid and with their philosophy of non-stop partying, I fit right in. Those days seem like a completely irrelevant bookmark in my life as I look back. I dropped out a year and a half after taking very easy classes and, frankly, being bored to death.

Six months after dropping out I was living in a small apartment in St. Helena with Nita, who I would soon marry. Believe it or not, she was still in high school. At 16 her parents had moved away to do missionary work on an Indian reservation in Arizona and pretty much left her to her own devices. I literally became her legal guardian at age 19 and we had our own little place in an old barn that had been converted into a five-unit apartment building, overlooking the most amazing vineyard and mountain landscape. She worked at the local A&W and I worked at the local pizza parlor.

—————————————

BELOW: The rest of my original family cast looks like this these days. I am on the far left being the standard class clown, then my sister Kate, brother Dave and Jeff and in the front mom Marge (with Toby) and brother Doug, shot at the family home just up the driveway from the Inn. All except Dave have had an active role in the Inn at one time or another.

Blackberry Refrigerator Pie

Inspired by Mrs. Gott

INGREDIENTS

10 graham crackers
(2½ by 5 inches)

1 cup sugar

5 tbls unsalted butter, melted

½ cup unsweetened
cranberry juice

2 Qts blackberries, (a few
whole berries reserved
for garnish)

¼ cup cornstarch

¼ tsp salt

½ cup heavy cream

DIRECTIONS

1. Preheat oven to 350 degrees.

2. In a food processor, blend graham crackers with 2 table-spoons sugar until finely ground; add butter and pulse until crumbs are moistened. Press mixture into the bottom and up the side of a 9-inch pie plate. Bake until crust is lightly browned, 12 to 14 minutes. Transfer to a wire rack and let cool completely.

3. Meanwhile, in a medium saucepan, combine ¾ cup sugar, cranberry juice, 2 cups blackberries, cornstarch, and salt. Using a potato masher, gently mash blackberries. Bring to a boil; reduce to a simmer and cook, stirring frequently, until very thick, about 1 minute. Remove from heat and let cool slightly.

4. Stir in remaining blackberries. Pour into cooled pie crust. Refrigerate until set, at least 4 hours (or up to 1 day).

5. In a large bowl, beat cream until soft peaks form. Sprinkle 2 tablespoons sugar over cream and continue to beat until soft peaks return (do not overbeat). Spread whipped cream over pie, leaving a 1 1/2-inch border around edge. Garnish with whole berries.

Steak Madeira

By Jim

Though I don't know what my father ate at those many dinners out with his clients, this recipe is certainly a nod to those days of carefree decadence. I have been known to add a little cognac while making the sauce to get a flambé going. After the first couple of times my wife suggested I stop, since it tends to splatter up the stovetop quite a bit and she seems to think it tastes just fine without all the showboating.

INGREDIENTS

2 1" thick or more Ribeye steaks
(my wife prefers New York,
my daughter, filet)

2 tbls clarified butter

4 cloves garlic, minced

A forkful or two of caramelized
onions (recipe later
in the book)

4 oz V. Sattui Madeira

1 tbl butter to finish

Pinch of finishing salt

A touch of Worcestershire Sauce
or Dijon Mustard if you're
in the mood

DIRECTIONS

1. Pull steaks from refrigeration at least an hour before cooking (room temperature).

2. Preheat heavy iron-cast skillet. Add clarified butter and when hot add steaks, searing to a deep brown on each side (depending on the thickness and starting temperature of the meat and how aggressive you want to get with the flame this can take 4 or 5 minutes per side. If you want your meat rare you might concentrate on browning one side deeply and then the other side you can pull whenever desired).

3. Add garlic and caramelized onions to the sizzling pan. Cook for 20 seconds or so.

4. Add Madeira and deglaze the pan, picking up all the chunks of browned meat and garlic and swirl in the caramelized onions. Reduce and add butter when the sauce is thickened. Pinch a little salt and add other ingredients as desired (my

wife hates this part because I can never recreate a dish she ends up loving): a couple spoonfuls of peach chutney, a splash of Balsamic, a scrape of nutmeg? And truthfully I run out of V. Sattui's Madeira because it's so good. (It's gotta be 15 blocks in the wrong direction for me making my way home.) Bourbon, good quality bourbon, works great in the recipe. You might have to add a decent splash of balsamic if you want to retain that sweetness, but that's what cooking is all about.

5. Let rest until the meat has sat for at least five minutes and serve with garlic mashed potatoes and broccoli (if you're looking for a bunch of great veggie or salad recipes you'll have to wait for my wife's book to come out. That might be a long wait).

NOTE: Since I mentioned chutney I have to tell you that I am a condiment junkie and there is nothing better than the chutneys that come from Bates & Schmitt out of Philo, California. The Schmitts were the original owners of The French Laundry, considered by many to be the best restaurant in the U.S. When they sold the restaurant to Thomas Keller they moved to a little apple farm in Philo. I don't know how widely these condiments are distributed but I have seen them in many specialty stores in California.

Steak Madeira

Sour Cream Sauce

By Marge

INGREDIENTS

1 part sour cream

2 parts plain yogurt

Nutmeg, vanilla and
sugar to taste

DIRECTIONS

1. Mix ingredients together and chill for an hour or so to let flavors marry.

This is a very simple recipe, but guests of the Inn have loved and commented on it for forty years. We serve it on fresh-sliced bananas with a little garnish of roasted sliced almonds or a sprinkle of our homemade granola. I have played with this basic recipe over the years, adding a little almond extract either with or without the vanilla, a couple twists of lemon and/or orange zest, things like that. All of my kids still love the original recipe and it is pretty much the only way I can get them to eat bananas even though two of them are fully grown.

Salami Roll-Ups

By Marge

This was a classic recipe back in those days that Chef Ryan has reinvigorated for our guests at the Inn.

INGREDIENTS

Sliced salami. I now use thinly sliced Genoa Toscano salami from the butcher's counter but I'm sure my mom used whatever came in the flat package in the deli section.

Jarred pepperoncini peppers, drained and patted dry

Softened cream cheese

Toothpicks

DIRECTIONS

1. Pull cream cheese out of the refrigerator at least an hour before preparing to bring to room temperature. Using a fork, soften cream cheese until silky smooth. You can add just a little mayo to help with this process but only after the cream cheese is well softened.

2. Remove peppers from jar and pat dry. Put a dollop of cream cheese and a pepper in the center of a slice of salami, roll salami and secure with a toothpick.

Though pepperoncini are the traditional peppers to use, why be stuck there. My larder is always filled with choices. Give me a minute and I'll go look. Yes; hot cherry peppers, marinated artichoke hearts, marinated red bell pepper (I canned those myself from last year's harvest), black Kalamata or Nicoise olives? And I didn't even look in the refrigerator! After all, were talking about pairing with a good salami and cream cheese, how can you go wrong? Place your filling of choice on a slice of the salami, roll it up and secure it with a toothpick.

Beef Bourguignon

By Marge

INGREDIENTS

10 sprigs parsley

6 sprigs thyme

2 medium onions,
    chopped coarsely

2 carrots, chopped coarsely

1 bulb garlic hit with a
    tenderizing mallet, peeling
    is not necessary. .

2 bay leaves

½ tsp whole black peppercorns

½ oz dried porcini mushrooms

6 oz thick-cut bacon, sliced into
    thick matchsticks

4 lbs beef chuck cut into 1 ½
    inch cubes

4 tbls butter

1/3 cup flour

2 cups beef or chicken broth

1 bottle red wine

1 tbls tomato paste

3 doz frozen pearl onions, Yes!
    Use frozen.

1 lb fun mushrooms.

A couple splashes of brandy

DIRECTIONS

1. The key to this recipe is probably quite different from the way my mother made it for all of her Napa Valley friends, but I would be remiss if I didn't alter the recipe to solve a problem I have always had with my stews. I love carrots in my stew but they are always either woody or mushy by the time everything else is perfect. So what I am suggesting is to put the first eight ingredients into a big pouch of cheesecloth so that you can infuse all those flavors without having them in the finished stew. So wrap them all up and put them in the center of your Dutch oven.

2. In a separate skillet, on medium heat slowly fry up your bacon. Since you want the grease (I always want the grease) cook at a lower temperature so that the bacon has a chance to release as much of its grease as possible before browning. Pull the browned bacon out of the pan and put it in your Dutch oven. Portion out the bacon grease so that you can brown your meat in the same pan in batches (if you put all the meat in at once it will release too much liquid and take forever to brown). Deeply brown the meat on all sides. Transfer browned meat to the Dutch oven. I usually run out of bacon fat at some point through this process and I would prefer using a little more oil than struggling to properly brown the meat. When all meat is browned

deglaze the pan with a little of the red wine and add that to the Dutch oven.

3. Add 4 oz of butter to the same pan. Once hot add flour and whisk together into a paste and brown until toasty colored. Gradually add in your broth and the rest of the bottle of wine (unless you have been sampling the wine as you go and have to open another bottle) and the tomato paste. I have never yet added too much wine to this recipe. When the mixture is thickened a bit add to the Dutch oven. You can certainly add some additional salt and pepper at this point if you'd like but I prefer a couple good shakes of Hungarian paprika, maybe even as much as a teaspoon.

4. Set oven to 300 and while the oven is preheating set the Dutch oven on the stovetop and bring your stew to a boil. Once boiling transfer to a middle rack in the oven and cook until meat is tender, about 2 ½ to 3 hours.

5. Remove Dutch oven from the oven and figure out a way to get the cheese-clothed veges out of the pot and into a strainer or colander where you can catch the juices and squeeze the veges to release as much liquid as possible. I use a strainer over a smaller pot and then push on the cheese cloth with my tenderizing mallet. Return that liquid to the Dutch oven and throw the veggies out. Take the same pot used to collect the juices and pull the meat out of the Dutch oven. Let everything cool.

6. While this is happening bring onions, butter, sugar, ¼ teaspoon salt, and ½ cup water to a boil in a medium skillet over high heat. Cover and reduce heat to medium low and simmer until onions are tender, about 5 minutes. Uncover and increase heat to evaporate all the liquid. Add the mushrooms and cook on high heat until mushrooms have released their liquid and all is browned and glazed.

7. While this is happening you want to appraise the brazing liquid in the Dutch

oven. It may well have a decent layer of fat rising to the top. Skim this off. The liquid may still be a bit thin and you are just about done so you may want to reduce it down to your finished consistency. I personally like the broth to be a little on the thin side so it mixes with everything else on my plate, but if you want the liquid to be more viscous now is the time to reduce it.

8. Once your sauce is reduced to the consistency you want it add the brandy, meat and onion/mushroom mixture back to the Dutch oven and heat until meat is reheated.

9. Serve over mashed potatoes (or my Winter Mash that will be described later) with a garnish of fresh parsley.

And then I wonder why my mother might have been reluctant to entertain while she still had to get five kids fed and tucked away while still making all the appetizers, sides and dessert! I just wouldn't do it if I didn't have a wife in there with me sharing the duties (plus we don't have five kids).

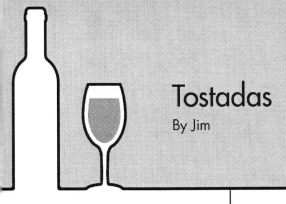

Tostadas

By Jim

INGREDIENTS

A few corn or flour tortillas (I strongly prefer 3 corn tortillas as a base, but if you want it to look pretty you pretty much have to go with one large flour tortilla so the edges stick out a little. Or, as my extended family does it they use Fritos Corn Chips as a base and call this similar dish Haystacks)

A little cooking oil (unless you use the Fritos)

A base layer of refried beans, taco meat, fried white fish or combination thereof

Build your favorite salad on top. Really anything goes, but ours have evolved from the traditional iceberg lettuce and shaved purple cabbage with a dollop of salsa and sour cream to mixed greens (no! not kale!!) with fresh cut raw corn, any color chopped sweet bells, sliced black olives, sliced zucchini, chopped onions (white, purple and/or green), shredded jack and cheddar cheeses (mixed 50/50) and your dressing of choice, or as my wife does it mixes catsup and sour cream for the topper.

DIRECTIONS

In college I lived on tostadas, both in Mexican restaurants and at home. Basically it was a fried flour or corn tortilla or two, a layer of refried beans, a bunch of salad piled on top with a little dressing and grated cheese. Nutritious, cheap and filling.

Of course today I have had to ramp these suckers up a bit. From the freezer I can almost always pull a vacuum-sealed "plate" of my Two-Day Taco meat, my Pepsi & OJ Carnitas or my Bacon-Bits Refried Beans. I call them "plates" because when I am finished making a big batch of any one of these recipes I portion them out into two-serving vacuum bags and after sealing them I shape them into flat plates so I can stack them high in the freezer. I figure if I cook a large batch of one of the recipes in this book once a month and freeze up what my family doesn't eat at the time I can have an amazing assortment of almost instant meals that are half an hour away from the table. I will give you all of these recipes (and many more) as you continue reading, but here is one you can try out to hopefully give me some street creds.

Pepsi & OJ Carnitas

By Jim

INGREDIENTS

3lbs pork shoulder, cut into 2 inch or smaller cubes

1 Qt bottle of Pepsi

1 Qt bottle of good orange juice

3 large onions rough chopped

20 to 30 cloves garlic

8 tbls chili powder

4 tbls cumin if desired (my wife doesn't care much for cumin)

Enough neutral cooking oil (or bacon grease) to brown meat after stewing

Salt to taste

DIRECTIONS

1. Place all ingredients except oil in a large stock pot and stew for a couple hours, until meat is tender. Let cool and separate the liquid from the solids.

2. Heat some oil in a large frying pan and (in small batches) add meat mixture and brown deeply. When fully browned add a portion of the liquid to the sizzling pan and reduce while deglazing the pan. This dish needs very little salt, but if you are going to salt it now would be the time. Repeat until all meat is browned and all liquid is reduced.

3. When you are done most of the meat will be shredded and some might still be in chunks. If you want it to be a stand-alone dish just treat it more gently in the pan to keep the chunks. I almost always use this dish as a filler for burritos, enchiladas or as a base for tostadas so I prefer to shred the meat while browning to make sure every fiber is browned and coated with the reduction.

CHAPTER 2

The Vision

The Wine Country Inn opened on August 15, 1975 with 14 individually decorated guest rooms, all decked out in antique furnishings, wallpaper or 100-year-old barn wood on the walls with accents of family-made stitcheries, along with family-made quilts for the beds. My parents, Ned and Marge, had infected the whole family with this new Bed & Breakfast craze and pretty much the whole family jumped into the project.

My mother quit her job as an elementary school remedial reading teacher to head up the decorating crew while my grandmother Nummy, my sister Kate and my then-wife Nita dove into the needlework. Later, when wallpaper and upholstery fabrics were being chosen, Mom drafted a neighbor, Sally Tantau, to help her with further decorating. My brother Doug, at age 23, was already a talented carpenter and woodworker so my father approached him to run the construction crew. Since somebody was needed to do the grunt work I was elected for that at age 21. Even my 12-year-old brother Jeff came in most days after school to sweep up the extreme messes that the carpenters always left behind.

Three generations of the Smith family were hard at work, with my father cracking the whip. And of course we all had friends who turned up on our doorsteps looking for work, all of whom had basic skills of one sort or another. Like me, I guess. I didn't have any actual training as a stonemason but that didn't stop my father. When it came time for the stone façade for the building, my father elected me as stonemason even though my training consisted only of working high school summers at the family's "ranch" in the wilds of Sonoma County (stories of this fabled place to come), building rock walls to flatten out garden plots or create a little parking.

My father's whole concept was to build something new that looked like it had been sitting atop this knoll in the middle of the Napa Valley for a hundred years. Dad insisted that all of the architects of his era were trained to design new, modern, sleek buildings. So instead, my father decided to hire another neighbor, Jim Hastings, who was a commercial artist and a bit of a history buff. Since my father had been selling real estate in Napa Valley for a few years he knew all the historic buildings he wanted Jim to amalgamize into this dream lodge. Soon the dining room table at the family home had been taken over, strewn with elevations (drawings of the exteriors) and floor plans. My father would bribe us all with free food and wine if we would come over and critique his creations. The passion he displayed for this new project was undeniable so I soon found that I had quit my job as a local pizza maker (they certainly didn't call us chefs back in those days) and instead could be found in a leaky, dark, dirt-floor barn breathing in stinky (and probably quite hazardous) chemical fumes

Brother Doug, friends Ron and Bill at Madrone Mountain

from the stripping goop I was using to bubble and peel old paint and varnishes from piles of antique beds, dressers and armoires my father had already collected long before he had rounded up the money and permits he would need to build the Inn. Spending the winter wearing rubber gloves, a little surgeon's mask and toxic chemicals, all alone in a cold drafty barn out in the middle of nowhere soon made me long for the warm pizza ovens.

The spring of 1974 arrived and my father had another brilliant idea. He had been out shopping for the rocks we would need to face the stone tower that he and Jim Hastings had designed and was now deciding that we should face the whole first floor.

It appeared to be way too expensive to buy the stone he would need, and, after all, it was just rock! Rock is everywhere in the Napa Valley. So he asked me to find a buddy to head out and pick up some rock; literally, his instructions were to drive around the roads in his old pickup truck and when you see a rock or two, jump out and throw 'em in the back! So we did. My best buddy Bill and I spent probably a

month cruising the backroads of the Upper Napa Valley "stoning." We drove around shirtless, with windows rolled down and long hair flowing, wearing beat-up jeans. Sometimes we would stop by the side of the road for half an hour, maybe longer, looking for rocks. Stoning was fun, but pretty soon my father figured out that free rocks were not so free (in fact the running joke among the crew was that my father would spend ten bucks to save one every time).

At that point my father decided to go big time. He rented (I can't see him actually renting something, so he more than likely called in a few favors instead) this beat-up ancient dump truck and sent us down to this gigantic pile of rocks that had recently been pulled from a huge vineyard that had just been planted down in the Stag's Leap District of Napa Valley. My father had sold this land to Carl Doumani and Carl had said sure, take all the rocks you want. Bill and I would head out from Lodi Lane at about 8:30 each morning, get set up at the rock pile by 9, spend three hours picking through this mountain of rocks, throwing the good ones chain-gang style closer and closer to the truck and then took one final heave up and over the side and into the back. We would head back to Lodi Lane around noon, dump the load, grab some lunch and head back for the afternoon load. We got two loads a day for about six weeks until, thankfully, the truck broke down. This mass-production style of rock collecting was not our idea of stoning.

Another sign of the times was that nobody was manufacturing vintage building materials in those days. Now you can go into almost any decent building material warehouse and purchase beautiful crown molding, pressed tin ceiling tiles, wainscoting in 20 different styles, and everything you need to make a new building look old. But back in the day, at least according to my father, these materials just weren't available. (They probably were, but they cost more than my father was willing to pay.) So, he sent me out with whatever buddies I could round up on another gleaning mission. My father knew of an old house that was being demolished on a piece of property he had sold to a friend who would soon become an investing partner. This friend gave my father permission to strip out whatever was reusable. To this day a number of the bathroom doors in the Main Building of the Inn came out of this old home (of course I later had to strip six or eight layers of paint off of them) and the wainscoting in a number of the rooms came from the tongue and groove ceilings that ran throughout this home.

A fun story came out of this escapade that I just can't imagine being repeated in these days of OSHA and liability insurance, but it was a story I told many times over when friends and students would ask me why I spent so many of my off-hours studying and teaching martial arts in one of the safest places anyone could possibly imagine. I was walking along one of the last ceiling joists of the kitchen of this house after knocking down the last of the ceiling material we were gleaning. I tripped on a protruding nail and suddenly found myself falling towards a floor strewn with the ceiling material we had just knocked down with all of the hundred-year-old rusted nails still poking out, ready to greet me in my fall. All I remember was that one second I was staring at a possible broken leg and certainly 20 or 30 rusty nails embedding at least an inch into my body to the next instant hanging from the joist that had been behind me. My buddies explained that I had screamed out some guttural nonsense (this was well before they had seen any karate movies) and swung my leg in a frantic sideways kick and had managed to turn myself around in mid-air to grab the joist, hang there for a moment before picking a safe place to land and dropping down without injury.

We decided not to tell my father about this escapade and went on to demolish two barns in addition to this house to glean some absolutely amazing barn wood that adorned the walls of a few of my favorite rooms until just a couple years ago when we switched the wood out for beautiful plaster work.

Soon construction on the Inn started in earnest, as the foundations were poured and the framing was starting to take shape. I don't know if any of you have ever helped carry 2 by 14 lumber, but those suckers are heavy. These were being used as the floor joists between the first and second floors and had to be nailed in at 16 inches on center. We spent what felt like weeks hefting these huge beams into place while the more skilled of us nailed them down. Since we had all the rock we would need for quite some time I had moved onto the carpentry crew — Bill had taken off for greener pastures since my father was only willing to pay him minimum wage which was something like $3.25 (hasn't gone up nearly enough in the last 40 years). This was long before pneumatic nail guns so I soon learned how to swing a hammer. I can't tell you how good it felt to develop a carpenter's swagger. To this day I can remember getting off work completely exhausted but still having the energy to strut the couple blocks to my house, tool belt slung over my shoulder like an off-duty sheriff of old heading home with two six-shooters easily at hand.

We were three quarters done with the building — framing completed, siding and roof on, sheet rock going up — when one of the crew came to my dad with a question, "I know that you worked out a deal with the neighboring community hall to use their bathroom while you were building the Inn, but where are the employees

going to go to the bathroom once the Inn is completed?"

I was standing right there, waiting for my next construction assignment. I think my brother Doug was there too. "Wha, what are you frick'n (my father never said "frick'n) talking about!! I am building fourteen bathrooms into this thing!"

"And you have fourteen guest rooms," whoever it was countered.

My father was floored, panicked even. "Augh!! They can frick'n use one of the guest rooms!!" he countered in desperation.

In the middle of construction we got the jack hammers out, blasted through the cement slab floor and connected a toilet and sink to the sewer line in what was already slated to be a too small storage room. Don't get me started on where we might launder the sheets and towels.

But none of this was much of a surprise for those of us raised by this, shall we say, frugal, man. As kids we lived in the town of Orinda until I was almost 12. Orinda is a bedroom community a half hour or so east of San Francisco (now with traffic it probably takes more like an hour). Maybe when I was six or seven my father bought a 120-acre "ranch" in northern Sonoma County. The ranch was up at the end of Dry Creek Road on a little side road called Skaggs Creek Road that would, if you stayed on it until it turned to a one-lane dirt track, pass through an Indian reservation and climb through mountains all the way to the cliff-laden Pacific coast somewhere between Gualala and Jenner (that is if you didn't get run off the road by a logging truck). Anyway, the driveway to The Ranch, being an off-shoot of an already very bad road, was truly terrifying. In good weather it was a slip and slide less-than-one-lane dirt track with pot holes the size and depth of the spare tire we would need more than once on our trips up. A forty foot cliff on the uphill side was complemented by a hundred and fifty foot cliff on the down side, a rushing creek at the bottom accenting the nightmare of venturing in that direction. But on a fully dark wintery Friday night in the pouring rain with my father out there sticking boards or rocks under the tires of our Ford station-wagon as we are stuck and fishtailing sideways towards the cliff, even our car-sick dog, Duchess Barf-on Cut-one, was whimpering from the fear oozing from the kids crammed into every nook and cranny of that car. Somehow we always made it and somehow my father never figured out that a four-wheel drive vehicle might literally be a life-saver at some point.

The real fun started once we got up to The Ranch. This isolated piece of property consisted of two cabins in the middle of the California Coast Range: rolling mountains dotted with magnificent oaks, whimsical madrones, and towering redwoods huddled in circular stands wherever there was enough water and protection from the blazing summer sun. And of course poison oak and rattlesnakes everywhere. The year-round creek that was our nemesis along the driveway coming up ran just behind the cabins and was our haven when we were allowed to play, but that seemed like only a brief and inconsequential interlude on these trips. Dad would always encourage us to bring friends along for these weekends, but we soon ran out of willing laborers for these cabins had been formally owned by — well — the biggest slobs ever known to man. The larger of the two cabins was really more like a three-bedroom house and I guess you could have called it a hoarder's house (we didn't have that name back then) but I really don't think they were actually hoarding anything since, at least to me, that would connote that any of the stuff was worth hoarding. But with the 20 or 30 cats that lived there and did their business among these piles upon piles of boxes and just plain crap, anything that might have been worth something was long ago not.

And that was just inside this house. Off the kitchen was a redwood deck that ran the entire length of the house, maybe 50 feet. To my recollection this deck was about eight to ten feet wide and about the same distance off the ground. I figured this out a few years later after we could actually see the far side of the deck and the ground below. Apparently these folks who lived here before us had been here for a very long time and every meal they had must have come from a can or a jar because every one of them was still here — and there — and over there, too. The length of their tenure could be determined by the dump sites that dotted the property. After a bit of exploring we postulated that originally these folks might have been somewhat fastidious, for they had taken their bags of cans, jars and bottles up the road a few hundred yards to dump them off one of the many cliffs. But then that must have gotten a bit too much because the dump sites kept getting closer and closer to the house until, well, by the end they couldn't make it even off the deck.

Now, in thinking back there could have been a number of modern ways to get rid of all this crap. A match and kerosene to the entire house could have been the most practical solution, after all it was a very nice building site. Or maybe a backhoe and dump truck could have been immensely useful. Or maybe, since my father had three little slave boys and one little slave girl (my youngest brother had not been born yet) we could all hand-dig huge pits, haul the enormous loads of trash over to them and bury it all! Oh, but no, the pits were too hard to get deep or wide enough to fit very much of the trash so, at the bottom of each pit one of us, the 7-year-old, the 9-year-old or the 11-year old, could stand and break every bottle and smash every can the rest of us had hauled over.

I think we worked on these projects for three or four years before we got off the deck and out of the kitchen. We were now into the really fun stuff because

My father with his crew. I'm holding Duchess, then sister Kate, brother Doug, friend Rick and brother Dave

the treasures in the living room and first bedroom were not only filled with dust and grime and spiders but they were also drenched in cat piss and mined with two-, five- and ten-year-old little bricks of cat crap. I remember we finally got to the bottom of all of this because I also remember taking some chemical formula to the floorboards of the living room that was supposed to remove to cat urine smell. It didn't work, but regardless, my father declared the house now inhabitable and instead of seven or eight or nine of us

(depending on how many friends we were able to con into coming with us) having to cram into the living room of the "little cabin," a one-bedroom 800-square-foot cabin that had been the mother-in-law's domicile and was actually somewhat livable when we bought it, the boys were sent down to the "big cabin" to sleep. I still have a hard-wired aversion to the smell of cat pee (and therefore the Napa Valley Sauvignon Blancs of the 1990s).

One of the real glories of those trips — other than indelible memories of sitting in the backseat of our station wagon, crammed between two brothers, in the middle of the night, during a torrential rain storm, absolutely certain I was going to die as we slid off the muddy road and plummeted down the hundred foot ravine, bouncing off trees as we fell — was making hand-churned ice cream. The ranch had an old abandoned orchard that we were trying to coax back to life and every summer we were able to harvest a couple bags of peaches, enough certainly to peel, slice and sugar to add to the vanilla ice cream recipe that seemed to be my father's only culinary achievement. My father definitely loved ice cream, but he also loved this recipe, not because of the flavors but because of the work involved in producing the finished product. It took a team, especially as the ice cream started to thicken. It took a tag-team of people to crank the tub, but it also took someone refilling the ice in the tub as it spun around, someone to sprinkle the rock salt over the new layers of ice and by the end of the ordeal it took someone to sit atop the tub so that you could get the final hundred cranks in — at that point switching crankers every ten or so turns — to really put the final thickening touches on the end product.

Fresh Peach Ice Cream
by Marge

INGREDIENTS

4 cups half & half

¾ cup sugar

1 tbls vanilla extract

1 tbls butter

6 large peaches, peeled and
cubed into ½ inch pieces

DIRECTIONS

1. In the morning add half & half, ½ cup sugar and vanilla to a mixing bowl and mix well until sugar is fully dissolved. Chill as cold as possible for at least 3 hours.

2. Add mix to an ice cream maker and follow the directions for that maker.

3. Peel and cube peaches. Sauté peaches in butter for half a minute and then add the remaining sugar (¼ cup) and cook until syrup forms.

4. Add peaches halfway through the ice cream freezing process. Enjoy when done.

BTW, it is still considered cheating in my family to use a motorized ice cream maker. After all, you have to justify all those calories somehow.

Whole Wheat Banana Nut Bread
by Marge

Here are two recipes of my mother's that I feel are iconic and helped set the tone for The Wine Country Inn: easy and comfortable.

INGREDIENTS

½ cup butter

1 cup all-purpose flour

1 cup whole wheat flour

2 eggs, slightly beaten

3 ripe bananas, mashed

½ tsp salt

1 tsp baking soda

1 cup sugar

½ cup walnuts, chopped

1/3 cup hot water

DIRECTIONS

1. Preheat oven to 325 degrees.

2. Melt butter and blend with sugar. Mix in beaten eggs and mashed banana until smooth. Sift all-purpose flour along with salt and baking soda. Stir in whole wheat flour. Add remaining dry ingredients alternately with hot water until all are just incorporated. Gently add banana/egg mixture, then chopped nuts lightly. Don't over mix.

3. Pour into greased 9"X5" loaf pan and bake at 325 degrees for 1 hour 10 minutes or until toothpick comes out clean in the center. Remove from pan as soon as cool enough to work with.

Baked Rome Beauties
by Marge

INGREDIENTS

12 Rome beauty apples

1 cup butter, softened or left out the night before

¼ cup brown sugar

1 cup walnuts or pecans, roughly chopped

1 cup apple juice

1 tbls or so freshly grated cinnamon

DIRECTIONS

1. Preheat oven to 325 degrees.

2. Core each apple, trying to leave the very bottom of the apple intact (this will act as a plug to keep the filling inside). You can do this with a little practice by twisting the apple corer just as you think you are about to punch through the bottom of the apple. Slice about half an inch off the top of each apple and puncture around each apple 6 or 8 times (like a baked potato, they might just explode without this step).

3. Mix all other ingredients except the apple juice in a bowl and stuff each core hole with the mixture, heaping a bit onto the cut top of the apple. Place in a deep baking dish, add apple juice to the dish and bake at 325 degrees for 40 minutes or until the flesh of the apple is fork-tender.

4. Serve hot in individual bowls with a splash of the juice.

This was a very special Christmas morning (or other family gathering event) treat. The remembered aromas are making my stomach ache as I write this. We still serve these at the Inn almost all winter long when other fresh fruit is not at its best. The cinnamon-apple mixing with the crackling fire and freshly brewed coffee equals comfort in the Common Room.

CHAPTER 3

Flash Forward

My mother will turn 90 years old during the writing of this story and can't really remember any of those filling and nutritious meals she used to prepare back in the day, but somehow all of her kids, four boys and one girl grew up with a love for good food, and I think all of us, with possibly the exception of my oldest brother Dave, have a love for cooking. I took my mom out for a drive recently to enjoy an amazing 85-degree November day in the Napa Valley. The leaves of the vineyards were just throwing off their most incredible displays of fall colors (as if they didn't give us enough pleasure from the fruit they produce) and I was asking her if she remembered what

Dad's favorite meal had been (he's been gone now for 24 years) or if she could remember any dishes I might be able to include in this story. She bravely searched back (she gets very frustrated at the things she can't remember) but couldn't come up with anything. We were on the Silverado Trail, heading south. There is a little rise at Mumm where the valley floor spreads out in front of you like one of the patchwork quilts my mother had made for the Inn when it first opened in '75. I could hear my mother catch her breath. Each block of vineyard was in a different stage of coloring. One block was still solid green, not yet ready to surrender to winter, one block was a dusty yellow and the next was full-on deep scarlet. Off in the distance the random displays continued as far as we could see.

I was thrilled to acknowledge that even though my mother could not remember the beautiful things that had filled her life, at least she could still enjoy life fully in this moment. We kept heading south, my mother commenting around every turn on the lighting the late afternoon brought to the checkerboard of colors or the new home (read mansion) snuggled just down from the road, intimate with the vines. "Halibut Florentine," I almost whispered it in reverence. "That fish guy that would come to the house, wasn't it on Thursdays?" My mother didn't look away from the vineyards but I could see her lips curl into a smile. "You'd fix it in those little scallop shells, I think it was the only way you could get some of us to eat spinach (not me though, peas were my nemesis)." She finally looked at me, this time with a little sparkle in her eyes, "Yes, I remember that. I put the shells on a bed of rock salt when I baked them so they wouldn't tip over." She looked back at the valley flying by, maybe embarrassed that that was all

she could remember and maybe grateful for the flashback moment.

At a non-descript unmarked little road I spontaneously slowed the car and turned left. If it startled my mother she didn't seem to mind. Of course she didn't recognize the road, split as it was into two lanes, the right lane up the side of the hill and the left still hugging the foot of the hill, giving as much room as possible on the valley floor for vines.

"Do you remember Carl Doumani?" I asked.

"Of course," my mother responded immediately, a little to my surprise. Carl was the first really big client (at least to my recollection) my father had snagged in the Napa Valley after he had quit his very lucrative job in the advertising business. In those days Napa's biggest agricultural product was beef cattle, the second I think was prunes and somewhere fighting for third and fourth were walnuts and grapes.

I explained how Carl had some years back sold Stags' Leap Winery (not to be confused with Stag's Leap Wine Cellars, that's a whole other story) and had built a winery on his remaining land called Quixote. And while my mother was correcting my pronunciation of Quixote we dropped down into a little side valley with Shafer Vineyards snuggled up on the hill to the left and a long row of trees before us that my mother was quite sure we shouldn't go down since there was a prominent sign declaring it was a private drive.

"I'll just grab their newspaper and take it up to them," I smirked. It seemed my mother's memory was coming back a bit because she actually giggled at the reference, for this was one of my father's favorite tricks. He was in real estate and he had five kids to feed. He couldn't just sit in his office waiting for clients to come to him. So, driving anywhere with him could always turn into an adventure. One of his favorite tricks was, when he saw a home or a ranch or a piece of ground that intrigued him we would pull over, he would grab the newspaper that had not yet been collected, drive up to the front door with the five of use slinking down as far as we could in our seats while he went and knocked on the door to "deliver the paper." Sometimes it would be a rather quick (terse? I wouldn't know, I was hiding) encounter, but more often than not it was a five or ten minute conversation with the startled occupant and possibly the occasional dip inside for a look around.

But in this case there was no newspaper in sight so I suggested Dad's standard back-up plan; we're lost and could use some help getting back to the main road. Of course my mother remembered that ploy as well so she smiled and relaxed. We headed up this tree-lined driveway with deeply shadowed yet brilliantly lit vineyards on both sides.

"Not a bad place to live, eh Mom?" Mom had been in a bit of a funk lately. In April we had been forced to move her into a care home in Calistoga and she was still missing that family home and the wonderful staff of caregivers (including my sister Kate) that we could no long afford.

"No," she admitted with obvious gratefulness seeping around the edges of her funk. "It's beautiful." Unfortunately Quixote is now almost completely hidden from the driveway and parking lot by its landscaping but Mom could get little sightings of the whimsical curving plaster walls with colorful ceramic tiles embedded here and there. She didn't want to get out of the car, so we drove up into the back and turned around at the crush-pad, still not seeing the true whimsy of this creation. It is tiny as far as wineries go and I launched into a story about how a general contractor friend of mine had tried to develop a bid for the construction of this building but he literally could not figure out how to construct all the angles and curves the architect Friedensreich Hundertwasser had come up with. I gave up on the story when I realized my mother was not really tracking so we moved on back down the tree-lined drive and pulled an almost complete U-turn where the drive had Y-ed earlier. Now we were headed up the drive to Stag's Leap Winery as I reminded Mom that one of Elvis Presley's last movies had been filmed here (or maybe it was Burt Reynolds). She had never been one for pop culture so that little nugget

also went sailing over her head, but the hundred-year-old stone building (once a very swanky hotel back in the horse and buggy days) caught her eye as did yet another breathtaking view of the vineyards, pleasantly framed by ancient walnut trees and stone walkways framing a stone and gravel patio. We could have as easily been in Saint Emilion, France, which was at one point St. Helena's sister city. I got out to take a couple photos while she sat patiently in the car drinking in the fresh air and sunshine.

After Stags' Leap we headed back north, back through the vineyards along The Trail with the sun dropping to the ridgeline, the symmetrical rows of vines whizzing by like some giant thumbing a deck of cards in your face. This is my favorite time of day and my favorite time of year in the valley. The rugged eastern hills show off their rocky cliffs with deep shadows behind stark outcroppings, directly above blocks of magnificent fall colors made deeper and more striking by the setting sun. This was especially true as we got closer to Calistoga. We call this eastern ridge the Palisades for good reason, a thousand feet nearly straight up, the rock promenades standing sentry over the valley.

Mom was quiet now, knowing she was close to the end of our visit. She seemed to sink deeper into her seat, diminished by the new reality of her life. And I was quiet, it was sad to think that she may well not remember any of this tomorrow. It was also sad to think that all those family meals might remain a clouded memory for me, not being able to conjure up the specifics of something I know my mother had taken great pride in at the time. We took the backroads through Calistoga and we sat for a minute or two in front of her new home in silence. There was nothing really to say at that point, the reality was that she was no longer capable of taking care of herself, but the worst part was that she was acutely aware of her frailties and equally aware that she still wanted more out of life. Finally, as we walked inside the home, the "escape" buzzer blared in our ears.

"You remember your homework?" I asked, placing my hand gently on her shoulder.

"Homework?" her voice squeaked a little. She was anxious and angry that I was going to leave her here and go back to my family.

"Remember, you were going to engage with Jean," When I got nothing but a couple quick nervous breaths from her and a little panic in her eyes. "Irais pulled me aside earlier today and said that Jean was sad when you weren't there for meals. She likes you."

"I like Jean," my mother grasped at the opportunity to understand.

"Jean likes you, Mom. She wants to get to know you better. Spend time talking," I was talking firmly, but was afraid to make eye contact. She knew her eyes gave her away and she was ashamed of her diminishing capacity.

"Jean hides a lot, she goes to her room," my mother seemed to be fishing for excuses now. She had never been extremely social, that had been my father's

job. I'm sure it was frightening for her to put herself out there like that, so acutely aware of her disabilities.

"She just needs an excuse, Mom. Just like you," hopefully I was being firm but compassionate. "Ask her to come watch a movie with you. I brought you all those movies. They're romantic comedies, easy."

"Alright, I'll try," she rallied and looked me in the eyes.

"I love you Mom," and gave her a gentle hug. "See you soon." As I walked for the door I was afraid she had already forgotten everything about her homework except the feeling of angst.

Two-Day Tacos

by Jim

INGREDIENTS

2 ½ lbs beef chuck

3 bottles good quality amber
or dark beer

¼ cup vegetable oil or bacon fat

2 large onions, coarsely chopped

8 to 10 cloves garlic,
coarsely chopped

6 bell peppers of any color,
coarsely chopped

3 Anaheim peppers, diced

2 tbls chili powder

2 tbls cumin

1 can stewed tomatoes or a few
big dollops of tomato paste
(either optional)

A little flour if thickening
is needed

DIRECTIONS

First off, I almost always double this recipe. Why go to all the bother if you're not going to freeze a bunch of it for on-the-go awesome meals? That means you should start with two six-packs of beer, one for the pot and one for the cooks. Also, I was always taught to dredge meat in flour before browning so that is what this recipe used to suggest (any recipe is merely a list of suggestions anyway, right?). Now I think, 'why am I browning the *flour* when I should be browning meat?' So if this dish needs a little thickening by the end either reduce it some more or make yourself a toasty rue and mix it in. Also when I first started making this recipe green bell peppers were not only the standard, but most of the other color bells simply weren't available. Last year the Inn grew 300 pepper plants in its garden and many of them were colored bells in red,

yellow, gold and a few green. So I doubled the amount of bells from the original recipe since six green bells would be overpowering, but mixing them can give you great complexity and a healthier dish.

1. So, brown the meat deeply in your oil of choice in a large stock pot.

2. Remove the meat and deeply brown the onions in the same oil, adding the peppers as the onions start taking on color and lastly throw the garlic in for the last minute or so.

3. Leaving the veggie mixture in the pot deglaze the pot with the beer. Add the meat back along with the rest of the ingredients.

4. Stew the meat at a simmer, uncovered for a couple hours or until meat is tender.

5. Remove pot from heat and when cooled a little remove the meat. Let both rest for the meat to cool and the fat to rise to the top of the broth.

6. Skim as much fat as you can from the broth.

7. Shred the meat with the grain, removing any chunks of fat or gristle.

8. Return shredded meat to the broth and reduce the broth to almost nothing, leaving yourself with shredded meat thickly coated with the broth reduction.

Halibut Florentine

INGREDIENTS

2 ½ lbs halibut steaks

3 tbls garlic butter

3 tbls flour

1 cup milk

Freshly grated nutmeg to taste

½ cup parmesan cheese

1 package frozen spinach,
    cooked and squeezed dry

½ lemon

1 cup mozzarella
    cheese, shredded

½ cup sharp aged
    cheddar, shredded

¼ cup panko breadcrumbs (Mom
    used regular breadcrumbs)

1 teas Old Bay Seasoning (or
    any number of other
    seasonings. I used a
    Jamaican Jerk mix recently
    and it was great)

DIRECTIONS

This is real comfort food for my mother. These days we are having it about once a month and I think my 13-year-old daughter Alura is finally starting to tolerate spinach when it is accompanied in this simple sauce.

1. Preheat oven to 350 degrees.

2. Melt garlic butter in a sauce pan. Add flour and cook on medium heat until the flour is very lightly toasted. Add milk slowly to make a basic white sauce. Add salt, pepper and nutmeg to taste. Add ¼ cup parmesan cheese. Reserve ¾ of the sauce. Add spinach to remaining sauce and mix well. Sprinkle generously with fresh lemon.

3. Mix the remaining cheeses, breadcrumbs and seasonings.

4. We still have the scallop shells Mom used to make this in so we layer each shell with the sauced spinach, halibut, more sauce and then the cheese and breadcrumb mixture to make individual serving shells.

5. Bake the shells at 350 degrees (on a bed of rock salt to keep the shells from tipping over) for about 20 minutes or until the cheese mixture is browned and bubbling.

CHAPTER 4

Learning on the Job

A few days before we opened the Inn we were making final preparations and my father casually asked me what I was planning to do once the Inn was completed. I don't remember if I had thought that far in advance, but I had recently gotten married, had a little apartment and most likely would need a continuing income. I remember shrugging and heading outside with the load of debris I was carrying, needing to unload it into the construction dumpster outside. It was probably 105 degrees that day and though hardened to the weather at that point when I came back inside my father's casual comment, "Why don't you help me run the place for a while?" struck a chord.

So, I guess I was the first employee of my father's new operation.

We didn't have a clue what we were doing when we first hung out our shingle. My father regularly shared his vision of having his feet up on the desk, leaning

Even our sign was handmade
by my brother Doug

back in a swivel wood-armed chair, maybe chatting with a potential guest on the phone (the single-line rotary-dial phone) and tossing an arriving couple a key while pointing them off to a room. That was not exactly the way it turned out. First of all, along with not envisioning an employee bathroom, I don't know that my father had actually designed a front desk into the plans. I seem to remember a rather frantic addition to the corner of the kitchen that my brother miraculously created in short order out of some of the barn wood we had left over from the rooms. And compared to the work my father continued to pour into the Inn if anything it was me who got to put my feet up on the desk. I still have this very strong visual of me working the phones, taking reservations and looking out at my 58-year-old father, pick in hand, digging irrigation lines for the landscaping sprinkler system, sweat pouring off his head and drenching his uniform — a seersucker shirt and khaki trousers — and loving it. There were many a time when I would try to shoo him outside after he had come in for a

drink of water because he was stinking the place up for the guests.

And we had no time to learn. We opened on August 15, 1975, in the heat of the harvest season with literally no other hotels in the Napa Valley besides a few motels in Napa, the El Bonita Motel in St. Helena and a variety of rather run-down lodgings in Calistoga, all associated with their own hot springs. And although it was still a year before "The Judgment in Paris" that would forever place Napa Valley on the wine maps of the world, a lot of folks were driving around looking for a place to stay. I should probably ask some of my father's original partners if he had ever presented them with a pro forma or a marketing plan, or god forbid, an operational budget for this investment, but if he did I never saw any of that. My recollection is that we opened our doors and two or three weeks later the phone (we only had one for the next ten or more years) was ringing off the hook and the rooms were full. And we were buying fans, lots of fans — for — you see — my father loved to sweat and he couldn't quite understand why others didn't love sweating as much as he. I'm sure it had something to do with being a Depression baby or the idea that real men sweat, but he knew the top floor rooms would get hot so he air conditioned the seven rooms on the top floor, but the middle and lower floor rooms all faced east so, since they didn't get any direct afternoon sun they should stay quite temperate. WRONG. Even at $33 per night folks were not happy with 90-degree rooms when they checked in with no way to cool them off. A hundred times my father was heard saying, "The Napa Valley cools off so nicely in the evenings. Within a couple hours it is going to be 50 degrees outside (which was true, but without leaving all their windows and doors open there was little chance that cool air was going to make in inside before three or four in the morning). We bought a lot of fans that first few months of operation.

In those days we served a very nice but rather Spartan

continental breakfast. We got the most amazing caramel pecan rolls from the Buttercream Bakery in Napa and my mother baked all sorts of nut breads at home and brought them in (nobody reading this works for the Health Department, right?). Banana Nut, Zucchini Nut, Pumpkin, Ginger Pear were just a few. We served an assortment of fruit and fruit juices. This was long before Odwalla or any of the finer juices you can get these days and my mother insisted on serving fresh-squeezed orange juice. My father, on the other-hand, insisted on not. I don't know how they ended up coming up with their compromise but I do remember on the evening shift we would break out this

little electric hand juicer and mix exactly half fresh-squeezed into the frozen juice we had already reconstituted. It really was pretty good.

But the real brilliance in my father's design for the Inn was the idea of putting private bathrooms in all the rooms. It may sound absurd at this point in Napa Valley hotel history, but we were the first Bed & Breakfast to open in the Napa Valley and though many followed in our footsteps none of them built new for many years and none of them had all-private bathrooms. This innovation kept us ahead of our competition for many years to follow. The other brilliance of my father's plan was to build his inn off the highway, out in the country with a view of vineyards and north of St. Helena where so much of the traffic turns around before heading back down south, back to the San Francisco Bay Area. But he paid a big price for that decision, for in those days financing for hotels was almost impossible to find, let alone for an untested area like the Napa Valley where cattle and prunes still far outstripped the tiny wine industry that was just getting a foothold. Tourists were

not interested in visiting cattle ranches or prune orchards and those tourists who did show up would certainly never search out some tiny lodging down some country road ten miles further up the road. So here, my father, a rather successful real estate developer in the area. was finding himself, hat in hand, kowtowing to self-important bankers with about as much imagination as a block of wood, looking for money for something he knew would work. He found no interest with the banks without sacrificing his core vision and now, honestly, there are hotels on every one of the locations the bankers suggested to him — on the highway, south of town. But in my opinion folks stay at these places in spite of their locations not because of them. My father was stuck yet again with a great idea and no way to fund it (I will explain this line later in the book). So he hit the cocktail circuit, talking to friends and colleagues until — $10,000 to $40,000 at a time — he put the money together that would fund his dream. And though we have enjoyed the greatest group of partners imaginable for the last 40 years I always lament a little that if my father had been able to secure a bank loan in the beginning we would by now be free and clear. Oh, well.

Now open, with guests flooding in, with paper and pencil we slowly (and with many mistakes) developed the tools to rent 14 individually decorated rooms, each quite unique from the next. We soon learned that when you describe a room in great detail to a potential guest and then don't take copious notes about what you promised AND be able to reference those notes at a moment's notice, you are likely to have some tense moments with your new best friends the Wilsons, or the Proctors or the Williams. You also soon learn the most intimate details about these folks that you simply never wanted to know: "I have never taken a shower in my life and I don't intend to start now," sticks out in my mind when an older female guest stormed downstairs after I had checked her into a room. The room only had a shower when she insisted she had been promised a bathtub. Or the gentleman who had insisted he had been assured he could reserve a room for just a couple hours and be charged half-price.

One of my favorite stories involved a very timid Japanese woman who came to the front desk. She wouldn't talk to me but fortunately we had a female at the front desk that day. "I think my husband is watching me," she murmured. When all she got was a puzzled look she tried again, "I think my husband is spying on me when, you know– when I am sitting — in the bathroom." As I think I mentioned, when building the Inn we had gleaned some beautiful wooden doors from an old house we had torn down. The doors needed new knobs, but we couldn't replace the old mortis locks that had been below the knobs and since we were just using them for bathroom doors in rooms that were designed for couples none of us even imagined there would be an issue. The holes through the doors were very small and as I say they were beautiful hundred-year-old wood doors, nothing we could have bought. My desk clerk was truly at a loss, she couldn't even grasp what the woman was talking about, but sure enough when the housekeepers went to clean the room the next day that tiny hole was crammed full of Kleenex.

Though some of these problems could not be solved with a pencil and paper, many of them could. My father and I soon developed systems to document and track most everything that happened around the Inn and when a new issue arose (still maybe once a week even after being opened for a year or so) we asked someone to watch the front desk and we would head downstairs and hash out a solutions so that that particular problem would never happen again. Truthfully the most repeated comment we got back then was that our rates were too low. I know I don't get that comment much (if ever) anymore, but that just goes to show that I can learn from my mistakes!

One of the biggest hurdles we encountered upon opening was where were our guests going eat dinner? As I mentioned earlier, the Napa Valley has not always been a Mecca for fine dining. In 1975 we had three decent restaurants in town at the time: The Abbey, which was a short walk away in the Freemark Abbey Winery building, La Belle Helene, a rather nice French restaurant, and some other kind of borderline place I can no longer

remember the name of. But I know there were three because they were all closed on Tuesday night. Upon realizing this, and sending folks to the really greasy-spoon Vern's Copper Chimney, my father immediately starting drawing up plans to build a BBQ station out on the deck of the common room. This was really an act of desperation because I'm pretty sure my father would have been able to put nothing on the plate but a charred steak and my mother wasn't about to start cooking side dishes for thirty people every Tuesday (let alone whatever the Health Department would have said to such an endeavor). But my father was nothing if not a problem solver. Within a few weeks of opening he approached Marc at La Belle Helene and convinced him that if he closed on Monday night instead of Tuesday night my father could fill his restaurant with Inn guests. Done deal.

It could be quite startling working the front desk back then. After we had been opened for two and a half very successful months when November hit the phone and walk-in traffic dried up as if someone had just built a massive dam upstream.

The phone traffic went from 50 to 60 calls a day down to 8 to 10 seemingly overnight and when a car drove up the drive my father would bolt (literally) out the front door. Within a minute or two he would have a couple entering the common room (sometimes dragging three or four feet behind, looking a little shell-shocked) to see a few rooms, at least for their next visit. Embarrassing, yes, effective, yes. For the first year or more the Inn sat atop a barren knoll, vacant countryside all around and an enormous pile of scrap construction debris my father refused to have removed because he was determined to make kindling wood out of it for the nine fireplaces he had installed. So outside the kitchen door he had set up a couple saw horses, a skill-saw and a heavy stump of wood with a large hatchet. Between phone calls or checking guests in the front desk staff could run out, saw a couple 8" lengths of fir 2 X 4s, pry out whatever nails might still be in them, then rush them over to the stump and with some mighty whacks from the hatchet split us some kindling. Fortunately, the front desk was in a corner of the kitchen so if a guest arrived we could sometimes see them coming, rush inside to wash up a little and still maybe be drying the sweat off our faces and necks before they got in the door. Other times the guests would come in the side door (known as the "sweat-heart door", story to follow) and the guests would not be so lucky. Though I don't remember any incidents around this directly I can certainly imagine hearing the little ding, ding of the traditional front desk bell alerting me to the guests' arrival and, hatchet in hand, sweat soaked shirt, red-faced from the heat, opening the back door to the kitchen and rushing in. Psycho and the Bates Motel come to mind.

I'll never forget the first t-shirts we had made to advertise the Inn. "The Wine Country Inn, For A Little *Peace* in the Country". They were just a little naughty so they flew off the shelves. My father's other little nod to what was going on in the rooms was his giggling insistence on calling the side entrance the "sweet-heart door." He repeatedly reminded those of us of the 'free-love' generation that things were not always that open. In his day (and it turned out still in the late 70s) there was still a very strong tradition of the man checking into the 'motel' and the woman waiting surreptitiously out in the car. It turns out my father had specifically designed the entrances to the Inn to allow for the woman to sneak in the side door and up to the room without being seen.

Our first major celebrity sighting went along with this theory at least to a certain extent. It was a typical Friday afternoon and I was working the front desk. A very suave man maybe a couple years older than I was came in to check-in. He announced the reservation was under the name of Head, Richard Head (but we could call him Dick). He filled out the registration card and paid for the one-night stay in cash. I went out to help him with his luggage and, wow, this woman stands up out of the passenger seat, head scarf, huge round sunglasses, and a form-fitting dress that accentuated the most luxurious hourglass figure I had ever seen. Though she didn't use the sweet-heart door she was certainly looking to be anonymous with those huge sunglasses covering half her face. I helped them straight to their room and then went straight to the rest of the staff to brag about the looker I had just checked into Room 5 along with this guy named Dick Head. We all kind of skulked around hoping for another glimpse, but it was not to be, at least not until sometime in the middle of the night. In those days one of the upstairs rooms was dedicated to the night desk staff. Two guys took turns either sleeping on the couch at the front desk to cover any emergencies or sleeping in the room upstairs. It turned out that night they were both down in the common room playing cards when the building-wide fire alarm went off. That sucker is loud! One of the guys, Chet, bolted to get ready to turn the alarm off while the other, Jay, started searching for the cause of the alarm. As guests throughout the Inn were either exiting their rooms or at least poking their heads out their doors Jay yelled out from the hallway of Room 5 that there was no fire, and that everyone could go back to their rooms. Dick Head was standing in the hall, shirtless but with a hastily thrown-on pair of pants trying to explain how he had tried to control the flame in the fireplace by closing the damper. All it had done was fill the room with smoke! At this point the smoke had filled the room down to about 3-feet from the floor. Jay took a deep breath, dropped as low as he could and bolted for the fireplace to open the damper. He took another breath from below the smoke line and managed to open the two windows before sprinting back to the main door to the room. On his way to the door he passed the bathroom vanity and there she was, the mystery woman, tiny baby-doll nightie covering at least a little of her lusciousness bending towards the mirror, reapplying her make-up. Upon passing Jay strongly prompted her to get out of the room, but all three guys waited for at least another minute for Jill St. John to stroll out of the room after finding the tiny frilly robe that matched her teddy. Jay and Chet reported the next day that they spent a very pleasant hour or so on the couch with Dick and Jill chatting and (appropriately) never letting on that they knew who she was. But secrets are hard to keep. Two days later an article appeared in the San Francisco Chronicle announcing that Jill St. John, hot off the set of the latest Bond movie, had been spotted with an unknown companion she had apparently met in Aspen. They spent a couple nights at the brand new Wine Country Inn in St. Helena before continuing their trip to Fiji, where they were expected to stay for a couple weeks. My father was thrilled with the mention in the paper but furious that someone on the staff had leaked this tawdry information. We all got off the hook when one of the kitchen staff explained that the gossip columnist who had written the story had also been a guest and that the next morning she had come into the kitchen asking for confirmation of her sighting. The staff member insisted he had given out no information and the whole incident just turned into another fun story.

Pumpkin Nut Bread
by Marge

INGREDIENTS

3 cups sugar

1 cup vegetable oil

4 eggs

1 ½ tsp salt

1 tsp nutmeg, freshly grated

2 tsp baking soda dissolved in
2/3 cup hot water

2 cups pumpkin, canned
or freshly steamed
and mashed

3 1/3 cups flour

1 cup walnuts, chopped

1 tsp cinnamon, freshly grated

DIRECTIONS

Makes 3 loafs.

1. Preheat oven to 350 degrees.

2. In a large mixing bowl add dissolved baking soda, sugar, oil, eggs and pumpkin. Mix well. Add remaining ingredients and stir until mixed (do not over mix).

3. Pour into greased and floured pans. Bake at 350 degrees for one hour and fifteen minutes or until toothpick comes out clean.

Poppy Seed Bread
by Marge

INGREDIENTS

2 cups sugar

1 1/3 cups vegetable oil

4 eggs

3 cups all-purpose flour

1 tsp vanilla extract

¼ tsp salt

1 ½ tsp baking soda

1 12-oz can evaporated milk

1 ½ oz poppy seeds

DIRECTIONS

Makes 3 loaves.

1. Preheat oven to 350 degrees.

2. Combine sugar, oil, eggs and vanilla in a large mixing bowl. Add in all remaining ingredients and mix. Pour into greased and floured pans.

3. Bake in 350 degree oven for one hour and ten minutes or until toothpick comes out clean.

CHAPTER 5

How Cool is Cool

I know that the Napa Valley is a very special place, but I don't really know how special. When I travel I tend to head for more tropical locales, so I have very seldom traveled in the U.S. It goes without saying that the Napa Valley scenery is spectacular and we are certainly world-renowned for our wines, but I wonder if all the other discoveries I have made about creating "the good life" could have been as easily made in some other town. Would I have figured out by running a small hotel in — say — Fresno or Tallahassee that I could have such a strong impact on peoples' lives; that by slowing my own pace and offering a truly friendly check-in and a room with a magical view instead of a television that

magical things could happen within my guests' lives? Or that the fulfillment I would get from witnessing those moments would add huge chunks of that "good life" to my own? I am thinking that living and running a small hotel in Napa Valley is way cooler than doing the same thing in almost any other town, but I could be wrong.

A couple quick stories. A few years after we opened I was working the front desk while Jill and Denise were cleaning up from breakfast service (the front desk was still in the kitchen at that point). Jill and Denise were two high school girls, full of giggles and playful energy (38 years later I still see one of them around town often). A man stomps in the front door and directly to the front desk. "You!

It was you!" he screams at me. The 23 year-old pimpled face behind the counter (me) was very glad there was a counter between us. The guy was big, and fit and purple-faced. "I need to know what you are going to do about this!"

The girls in the back freeze, childish grins melting from their faces. Then shock fills their eyes and I think some real fear as a very lovely woman rounds the corner about bursting with child. "You did this," the man keeps up.

"I, I," I stammer.

"You and your Inn," he continues, evolving only slightly until neither he nor his lady can keep the smiles from their faces any longer. "We have been trying to get pregnant for three years and you did this!" suddenly joyful in celebration. He then reaches across the front desk podium and, though I'm sure I flinched, manages to grab both of my shoulders, grab my attention with his eyes and says, "Thank you."

I doubt that I teared up at the moment, but I am tearing up a little now at the writing of this. How many people, in their chosen profession get moments like that?

While I'm on a roll, I'll tell you another. Jimmy Messina may not be a household name to all of you, but I knew who he was when he checked-in. He had played with Stephen Stills and Neil Young in Buffalo Springfield and later went off to have pop success with Kenny Loggins. I think this was after all those days, but he had checked in to search out wines for the empty cellar in the house he had just bought. One afternoon he had finished up his touring and had plunked himself down at one of our common room tables, sheet music strewn about, apparently working on some new tunes. There were two of us in the front desk/kitchen area peeking around the corner, trying not to disturb him, but giddy with excitement. I think I even took the phone off the hook and for some amazing reason the way I remember it no one even walked through the common room or up to the front desk for a good long time until this young couple strolled in and went over to sit in the couch by the crackling fire. I can't remember who was there with me, but we were both worrying that this new intrusion might ruin the moment. Jimmy continued to play, mumbling words and experimenting with cords. More stretched moments passed but it turns out Jimmy was not oblivious to the couple at the fire, apparently he had been watching them. He stood up with is guitar in hand and walked over to sit across from them in front of the fire. He probably knew already just from their posture and their seeming self-absorption that they were on their honeymoon. Jimmy sat for easily half an hour and serenaded them before excusing himself to get ready for dinner.

I'm guessing that these stories could have occurred at any small hotel in any vacation spot. People are just different on vacation and that's why vacations are so important to all of us, but to be a part of those moments and a million smaller ones that share that same spirit — well — it is a magical way to make a living. Those moments are a huge part of the "good life" for me and though I forget to thank my mother and father for this lifestyle they have afforded me I should.

Napa Valley has to be a special place for a foodie as well. I don't know this,

but I am guessing there aren't very many places in the U.S. where you can go to a Farmers' Market and learn that there are not three different kinds of garlic like I was taught during my culinary training, but hundreds, some of which being the most beautiful works of nature I have ever seen. Garlic is grown all over the world and the variety of flavors, skin colors and potency are truly staggering, but if it hadn't been for a sweet and frail older woman with a tiny stand at our local Farmers' Market with an even tinier display of her wares I never would have discovered how limited our lives can be when it comes to the many culinary delights you can find if you look for them.

I truly should have already known this because for years after returning from a six-month trek through South America when I was 19 I told the stories of the street markets where, much to my confusion and disappointment (since I didn't have a kitchen to experiment or friends with me who had the least interest in my discoveries) I found literally dozens of different kinds of bananas available for purchase, and then peppers in every color, size and shape and then carrots, same thing, rainbows of brilliance. Then there were whole stalls of leafy greens or root veggies that I could only guess at their uses or flavors (we were living on $6 per day and my traveling companions had completely different priorities). When I eventually got home to St. Helena I was known for years to rail on the pathetic selection of vegetables available in the U.S., but to be honest it was more of a self-important bitch (I knew better) than a real desire to search new flavors out and experiment with them.

I know that Dean & Deluca started in New York City, but to have one of its satellite stores in a market that serves a few thousand customers instead of one that serves millions, I feel blessed. For those of you who do not have this experience on your radar, you are missing out. Though there are other amazing culinary stores that have cropped up I still think that Dean & Deluca has, by far, the best trained staff, and that really goes a long way when looking for the perfect little morsel of food. I can tell you two stories about this amazing store, both date back a few

years to when I was a single man in my late thirties and early forties. I wandered into Dean & Deluca after it had been open for about a year. I was just kind of browsing around and found myself in the cheese, pretty much overwhelmed with the selection. A pretty young lady approached me from the other side of the counter and asked if she could help. I admitted to her (Alice) that I had spent two years studying the culinary arts at San Francisco City College (at that time considered one of the best two year programs in the country) but that I was completely ill-prepared for what I saw in front of me. She smiled and asked what kind of cheese I was looking for. Of course I didn't know so I punted. "Nothing too stinky, but I love the soft ones, the creamier the better." I think she was shocked that I had been to a top-rated culinary school and that was the best I could do.

"Let me have you try this," Alice suggested after searching the counter for a while. "This is a winter-milk cheese. I can only get it this time of year and by next year we won't be able to get it at all, it's not pasteurized." She unwrapped this

Dean & Deluca Cheese Display

the owners showed up four or five times a year for three or four days but needed everything to perfection upon their arrival. Alice explained over the next couple of months (we dated a bit) how Dean & Deluca had hired her straight out of The Culinary Institute of America in Hyde Park NY, worked her in the New York store to make sure she had potential and then sent her to France for six months to study cheese — all expenses and salary paid. It turned out that after a thousand or so years the Europeans had learned a thing or two about making cheese (things that either had never made it to the U.S. or things our cheesemakers had just rejected in favor of cheaper and/or faster). You'd think that would be obvious, but it wasn't to me. At San Francisco City College our instructors had insisted that parmesan cheese was merely dried jack cheese, and indeed, in 1979 when I was getting my culinary education

soft-rind snow-white delight and cut me off a little taste. I'm not great at describing flavors (or remembering them 20 years later) but I remember a complexity and full-mouth experience with just a hint of stink.

"Winter-milk?" I asked.

That launched us into a full hour and a half tasting extravaganza that I will never forget. It turned out this young lady was a private chef for one of the original family members of John Deer or International Harvester or something and she lived in this huge mansion with the housekeeper and the gardener, where probably 99 percent of American parmesan probably was! Along with a million other cheese-facts I learned that the milk the cheese is made from is paramount to the finished flavor of the cheese. If the cows (or other animals) are grazed on lush green winter grass the milk (and therefore the cheese) is going to taste completely different than if the cows are eating dried hay. Rinds, aging, cultures, herb additions, soil types and climate — we covered it all, hanging out in this echoing mansion among 40-year-old cabernets and crystal goblets that were strictly off-limits to us. My appreciation for the U.S. food-supply industry took another major hit.

The other Dean & Deluca story involved putting a picnic lunch together for when I was dating my future wife Lorinda. We were heading over to the coast and I wanted to stop halfway at Armstrong Woods, a most amazing park of coastal redwoods (I should probably do this again real soon, ya know, keep the magic alive). Anyway, I was strolling around Dean & Deluca (Alice had been transferred to their Charlotte North Carolina store) and I had picked out most everything I thought

I needed for this seductive lunch, but I still needed a little fruit (Lorinda is quite sporty and I had not yet corrupted her to the dark side of fatty cold cuts, triple-crème cheeses and such). I wandered into the produce department with the general idea that I needed an apple or two.

"May I help you?" asked a young man who was loitering around the produce section. He probably had a store shirt or apron on, but I still probably frowned at him a bit. Produce is something I figured people seldom need help with. But then I remembered back about the cheese. And being almost completely lacking in personal boundaries I proceeded to tell this stranger my plans of seduction under a 200 foot redwood canopy. Things immediately got serious. Flip, a knife appeared in his hand. "Come check these out," he walked over to a display of some roundish white-yellow apple-sized fruit. This started a forty-five minute extravaganza of fruit tasting. This kid was evangelistic. After he would cut into some pear or apple obviously he couldn't sell it so he would give me a taste and then hit up the next ten people walking past to coerce them into tasting as well. Soon there were a few of us customers just kind of hanging out while he held court, running around like a maniac with knife in one hand and local fruit in the other. I took so long picking the two apples I was looking for that I was late picking up my date. Fortunately she married me anyway.

»————————«

Update: It's hard to believe, but after I wrote the above stories I realized they took place almost 20 years ago and though I have been into Dean & Deluca many times since then I usually know what I want when I go in and so I don't really "test" the staff like I did in those stories. So last Saturday I made the executive decision (yeah, as if that would have worked if it hadn't been something so fun) that my wife, daughter and I would head down there in the late morning to see if the service was still as awesome as it had been. I told my family before we went in that I really wanted to push the staff a little and they were up for it so even though we had other fun staff planned for

that day we just kind of cooled our jets and strolled to the cheese counter. They had a few pre-cut tastings out, but even Costco does that these days. We kind of browsed around a bit before anyone paid attention. Finally a matronly woman asked us if we needed help. I gave her a whole spiel about how my daughter liked a full-bodied harder cheese with a bit of a tang. The woman looked a little stumped, but the question got the attention of another woman behind the counter and before long I was looking at a two-year aged Manchego all saran-wrapped and ready to take out the door. I tried to smell it as she waited expectantly for my reaction. "Can we taste it?" I finally prompted her, more than a bit disappointed that she had merely expected me to take her word that this was the cheese I was looking for.

She seemed to come out of her stupor a bit. "Well — of course," she said, not really reluctantly, yet not really enthusiastically either. She unwrapped the cheese and gave us all a taste without any kind of story of winter milk or towns in Northern Spain which Alice would have done. We finally warmed this woman up, especially after I told her that my 13-year-old daughter had recently announced that she wanted to be a chef when she grew up, and the other woman behind the counter chimed in occasionally, so all in all we did ok, but they would probably do as well at Whole Foods or our local Sunshine Food Mart. We then went to the produce department and being the dead of winter there were only a few choices. The saving grace for our visit was two-fold. First when we got to the cold-cut department the same woman followed us over and this seemed to be much more her thing. We got into a long discussion about chorizo and how, in Spain, every town has their own version of chorizo that they have been making for hundreds of years. This was welcomed information to me because though I had tried a couple Spanish chorizos (more like a salami than the disgusting Mexican chorizo I was originally introduced to forty years ago) and I liked them, I now had a whole new research project to add to my studies of the world's paprika (a whole other story).

The second saving grace was that I wandered into the hard liquor department. There I met Brad and we started talking booze, and more specifically tequila. I pretended I was new to the subject (which I am not) and let him yammer on about soil and climate and altitude and distilling methods and it was very clear he was well-trained and enthusiastic. I then started noticing the very nice selection of gins, and though gin is not my poison of choice I do enjoy a good martini every once in a while and I noticed some different colored 209 gins, so I asked about those. It turns out that a number of gin makers are experimenting with aging gin in previously used wine barrels, giving the gin a pink shade. Needless to say I walked out with a new brand of tequila I was dying to try and one of those pink gins that a buddy of mine and I tried a few nights ago and *yeah, it's gooooood!*

So, all-in-all it is this a great experience, but I'd say they better step up their game if they want to remain #1.

Oakville Grocery was Napa Valley's first foray into the gourmet food arena (before Dean & Deluca) and for years I used to stop in there nearly every time I passed, and though it is still an interesting store I can get near everything I would be interested in from this store at our amazing Sunshine Foods grocery store in St. Helena. For a general grocery store ("general" meaning they have most everything you would need on a daily basis, not "general" as in "regular") Sunshine is spectacular. My only problem is that I can never just duck in there to get a few quick items. Having lived in St. Helena for fifty years now I am bound to run into at least five good friends and wave and smile at another ten. I doubt this story will be complete without delving into my love affair with bread so I'll probably get back to talking about Sunshine at some point in this story, but if I forget, make sure to drop in the next time you are in town. It is worth exploring.

The Olive Oil Manufacturing Co is a little barn at the end of Charter Oak that no longer makes their olive oil right on site but is another local delight that is truly unique. Again, before Sunshine Foods got so interesting this was a weekly stop for my explorative grocery education (that almost sounds like work). When my kids were little I would have to leave them outside at one of the picnic tables because they wouldn't even go inside with me, the wafting cheese smells exuding six or eight feet out the wooden screen door were just too much. Unfortunately the local Health Department has completely ruined that part of the experience (all the cheeses are now refrigerated and hermetically sealed which I think, sorry Janahia, is so wrong), but for experimenting with wide ranges of salami, olives, cheeses, olive oils and condiments it still can't be beat. In fact I have a new favorite that I hesitate to mention because I figure at least a few of my friends are going to read this book. A few months ago I was in there buying my two-week supply of EV olive oil and a hunk of their amazing Teleme cheese (it's kind of a mild super creamy whole-milk jack that apparently a lot of the local Italians use as "risotto cheese"). I just like it for parties for those friends who don't want a big stinky cheese messing with their breath. Anyway, Ray, the son of the owners and the guy I have been buying cheese from for at least 40 years, comments, "ever serve that with our olive oil drizzled over the top and a little fresh cracked pepper?" Well crap! I now have a brand new nemesis to my waistline! Holy shit! With a little Acme sourdough batard! But friends and neighbors, if you're going to rush over and give this a try, remember, this is a special cheese made over in Sonoma somewhere (not like any other Teleme I have ever been able to find, and I have tried) and they don't make much of it, so if you are grabbing the last hunk, think again and remember who brung you to the party!

So, am I just being overly proud? Do most communities have these kinds of resources where daily discoveries are so amazingly in-your-face possible? It seems everywhere I turn in my hometown, forty years after opening my eyes to the possibilities, new experiences just keep popping up in front of me! I think what has really made THE difference in St. Helena is the protectiveness of its citizens. Napa has a Whole Foods and a Trader Joe's and some other great spots like Genova Deli and such, and, thank God, Santa Rosa has a Costco for my bulk shopping, but St. Helena has my soul. I can't tell you how disgusted I get

when I travel through California and see nothing but strip malls, box stores and chain restaurants. We were able to keep all of that out of St. Helena. I am a little embarrassed to say that the only two "chain" businesses we have in St. Helena, Safeway and A&W were both brought into town by my father back in the 60s. After my father built the closest thing we have to a strip mall and helped our local mayor at the time bring in A&W the locals read the tea leaves and promptly passed some Draconian ordinances to keep the rest of the hordes out. And though, because I am in the "tourist business" I was for years ostracized from a few of the local bars by who had been good friends in high school, the overall effect of their rabid protectionism has been our saving grace. I just got a call from my nephew who lives outside of Austin, Texas, who says his little town is about to be gobbled up by box stores and chain restaurants and asked how we had done it and the only answer I could give him was to be a major pain in the butt every single time anybody wanted to do anything that smelled of change, even if you couldn't make even the smallest connection between your feelings and a logical argument.

I can't tell you what all this means to me. Every morning I walk out of my probably hundred-year-old home, walk through a neighborhood of mixed architecture with a few picket fences,

Even in winter I have a special place to walk.

some with lawns, some without, before veering off onto a path that takes me out into the vineyards for a two-mile walk to the Napa River and back.

Ok, so yes, I know this place is special, but how many of my life discoveries are worthy of putting down on paper (and trying to sell them to an unsuspecting public)? My daughter, who actually convinced me this kind of book would work, thinks there are many, but I am not sure. It feels extremely self-indulgent, but I guess if you've read this far through this book maybe I can take a chance and keep indulging myself.

Thinking back about the discussion I ended up having with the last woman I talked to at Dean & Deluca it reminded me that I have a great recipe for Mexican Chorizo that I haven't made in a while (Chef Ryan makes at least one batch of this recipe every week for various recipes we have at the Inn). It's funny, because there are two reactions I get from people when I tell them I make my own Chorizo. The first is kind of a blank stare and I realize they are thinking about that God-awful stuff you see in the chain grocery stores that comes in a plastic casing, is 50% fat and who knows what the other 50% is.

Yuck! The other reaction is, "What do you use for casings?" These both seem to be perfectly good excuses not to make your own Chorizo, or any kind of homemade sausage for that matter. But that just isn't the deal. I don't put any of the sausage I make into casings. Half the time when I am using store-bought sausage I am making a recipe that calls for taking it out of the casings anyway. And secondly, when I make my own sausage I can totally control what I put in it. I can control the quality of the meat, the fat content and I can fine-tune the flavors to precisely what I like. I will give you the recipe for my Italian Sausage later in the book.

Mexican Chorizo Sausage

by Jim

INGREDIENTS

3 lbs pork shoulder (ground pork makes the process a lot easier but then you are losing some of that control, but for the first few times you might want to just use ground pork)

¼ cup olive oil (omit if using ground pork)

15 to 20 cloves garlic, minced

1 tsp gray salt, if you've got it

1 tsp cayenne pepper, ground

2 tbls cumin, whole

1 tbls cumin, ground

2 tbls pepper flakes

3 tbls paprika

3 tbls chili powder

1 tsp black pepper

½ cup red wine vinegar

DIRECTIONS

1. Cut pork into 1 inch cubes, removing as much fat as you feel is appropriate.

2. Add meat and olive oil to a food processor and pulse the blades until meat is roughly ground.

3. We like to toast all the spices before adding them to the meat. In the skillet, place all spices over medium heat and toast until aromatic.

4. Add all ingredients to the food processor and pulse until well mixed.

5. Set aside at least overnight before adding to your favorite recipe.

On another note, because of all of the amazing places to shop in the Napa Valley I have become a total condiment junkie. Given that I grew up in the '60s with tons of my friends coming back from the Viet Nam War I would count myself lucky that this is the kind of junkie I became, but my overcrowded larder might not agree, the shelves are literally sagging from the weight even though I use a lot of it regularly. I simply can't go into any nice grocery store without finding myself in the isle with the vinegars and chutneys and BBQ sauces. But boy does my collection make throwing a quick dinner together an easy thing.

Homemade Refried Beans

by Jim

There is absolutely no resemblance between canned refried beans and these. They freeze well, so this recipe will make a large batch. Then anytime you would normally be pulling a can of beans out of your larder you could as easily pull a zip lock bag out of the freezer.

INGREDIENTS

1 small bag pinto beans

1 large onion

2 tbls cumin

2 tbls red chili powder

2 tbls paprika

1 lb smoky bacon

10 or more cloves garlic

Salt to taste at the end

DIRECTIONS

1. In a large pot cover beans with 4 or 5 inches of water and soak overnight. Drain and rinse the beans when ready to cook (they always say to pick out any rocks or clods of dirt, but I have never found any yet).

2. Cover again with water and simmer with onion, garlic and uncooked bacon until beans are tender. Add spices. Continue to simmer for another couple of hours or until beans start falling apart and liquid has reduced substantially (yes, you are overcooking them).

3. Transfer hot beans and remaining liquid to a hot non-stick frying pan (I usually have to do this in batches). On high heat fry the bean and liquid mixture (maybe add a little extra bacon grease if you have it) while mashing them into a smooth(ish) mass. Brown the beans, mix and brown some more. You can always add a little water if they get too dry before they are browned. Salt to taste.

Chicken Breast Bake

by Jim

INGREDIENTS

3 or 4 plump bone-in chicken
    breasts, should be enough
    to almost fill the bottom
    of the pan you are
    cooking them in

A sprinkling of olive oil

½ can of chicken broth

1 jar of whatever jarred delight
    you might have: peach &
    almond or fig & walnut
    chutney, cranberry-bourbon
    confit, cinnamon-pear
    jam just to name a few
    things I just pulled from
    my cabinet.

DIRECTIONS

1. Preheat oven to 350 degrees.

2. Heat oil in cast iron skillet and sear chicken skin-side down until deeply browned. Turn chicken bone-side down and add chicken broth, heat a little, then add your jar of yumminess.

3. Throw in oven for 15 or so minutes until chicken is cooked through.

4. Serve with a mixed green salad and some grilled crusty sourdough bread.

Kick-Ass Sea Bass

by Jim

INGREDIENTS

¾ lbs fresh Chilean Sea Bass

Flour, enough to dust Sea Bass

1 tbls clarified butter

½ onion cut in thin strips

1 cloves garlic, minced

½ cup port or other sweet wine
or liqueur like Cointreau
or my new favorite,
Patron Citronge

DIRECTIONS

1. Preheat oven to 400 degrees.

2. Pat Sea Bass dry with a paper towel and dust both sides with flour.

3. Heat butter in a cast iron skillet on high heat. Add Chilean Sea Bass to the center of the pan and the strips of onion around the outside. Brown fish deeply on both sides while browning the onions at the same time. Turn heat off for half a minute and add garlic for a few seconds before adding the liquor. Make sure the fish is separated from the pan and onions are stirred into the liquid. Place in oven to cook fish through (about 10 minutes). In my opinion Chilean Sea Bass is nasty unless cooked thoroughly.

Note: Chilean Sea Bass is the only fish I have found that can stand up to this kind of abuse. Unfortunately when I first developed this recipe this fish was plentiful and cheap. Now it is over-fished and ridiculously expensive. But my wife still requests it now and then so the recipe has stayed alive. It is great with Italian Red Rice and since the oven is already being heated might as well throw in some oven-roasted Brussel sprouts a half hour before you put the fish in. Oh, now you want the recipe for the Brussel sprouts? Okay.

Oven-Roasted Brussel Sprouts

by Lorinda

INGREDIENTS

1 lb Brussel sprouts, cut in half

½ cup or so good olive oil

A couple good splashes balsamic vinegar

4 to 8 large cloves garlic, minced

¼ lb bacon, fried and chopped to bits

¼ lb parmesan cheese, finely grated

DIRECTIONS

1. Preheat oven to 400 degrees.

2. Parboil Brussel sprouts in boiling water for seven minutes. Drain into colander and dunk into ice water to stop the cooking.

3. Place drained Brussel sprouts in a greased baking dish and toss with oil and vinegar. Place in hot oven and roast for 20 minutes, stirring only occasionally to let browning develop.

4. Add garlic, stir again to spread around. Roast until sprouts are tender but not wilting.

5. Pour into serving platter (or keep in baking pan) and garnish with bacon bits and cheese.

CHAPTER 6
Many a Family

Five days after my 22nd birthday I found myself as Assistant Manager of this brand new business. As previously mentioned I had dropped out of Chico State after a year and a half to take that six-month trek through South America and hadn't seemed to find my way back to college. My brother Doug, who had been the building contractor for the Inn took off for other building projects (he would come back for our expansion in 1979 to build the Brandy Barn and Hastings House). My mother, who was still the decorator, stayed active in that field up until very recently and additionally helped develop the Continental Breakfast we served at the time. She also had a big hand in developing the landscaping of the Inn (handing my father the pick and shovel, which he loved), but other than that she never got involved in the actual operations. My brother Dave had moved to Berkeley a few years before the Inn was even conceived of, so he was not involved. My sister Kate soon moved to Los Angeles to pursue a career in the music business and would many years later return to the Inn as our elopement coordinator and interior designer for a number of years, taking over for my aging mother. And brother Jeff was only 12 when the Inn opened and would eventually work as a night clerk for a while during high school, but other than that had other interests (mainly as a punk rocker in the early 80s — so much so that I remember having to have a little talk with him about coming to work with his stage make-up on. I told him he could put it on in the bathroom on his way OUT from work but not on his way IN to work).

This left my father and me to figure out how to run this fledgling business. I remember so clearly my father, a little bit joking and a little bit not, saying, "How tough can it be? You put your feet up on the desk, talk on the phone a bit and when someone comes to check-in you throw them a key after greeting them with a hearty welcome." Yeah right!! For the first year I can still see him, his ears perking up as he hears a car coming up the driveway, his eyes glued to the window where he watches the car park. But if it doesn't park, if it tries to pull a u-turn and head back down the driveway Dad is out the side door, through the side gate, flagging the simply curious driver down. Nine times out of ten within a couple minutes Dad is walking them in the front door for a little tour and maybe some lemonade.

True, the Inn was built with a huge effort from my family, but much of my family had now moved on so, though it wasn't by design it seemed logical that we would not have objections about other families becoming involved. I guess I could focus on all the conflicts and complications this philosophy caused, but I'm just not that kind of guy. The reality is that the family connections, whether they be the original Smith family or the many other families that have helped us since then, have added an irreplaceable richness and authenticity to the Inn and have made this an even more special place.

>>————————————<<

The McGrath dynasty was the first of these families to get involved. Mr. McGrath (his first name is Chuck, but since I was in my early twenties and he was like ancient, probably 50, I think he remained Mr. McGrath to me) and his wife had nine children and one of his middle children, Kathleen, was a close friend of both my wife's and mine. I don't remember where she started in the organization, but Kathleen soon showed her abilities as a dedicated and talented member of the staff and was promoted into the office as our first bookkeeper. Within a year Kathleen's father had been hired as our first handyman, I think all three of the triplets worked with us at one time or another in housekeeping and the kitchen, as well as Maureen at the front desk and Joe in the gardens. My wife and I were in Kathleen's wedding to Rich who was an original member of the masonry crew and had continued on with us, continuing with a huge number of landscaping rock walls as well as working as a night clerk for the overnight shift. He lived on property and eventually became the foreman of the masonry crew for the construction of the Brandy Barn and Hastings House. When I went off to San Francisco City College to finish up my degree in Hospitality Management my father promoted Kathleen to Manager. When I returned from school and took my father's place at the helm Kathleen and I enjoyed another few years running the Inn before she moved on.

»————————«

Margarita Espinoza was a good friend of Kathleen's and Kathleen hired her as our Head Housekeeper. I couldn't really remember all the different relatives Margarita had hired so, for the research for this book I thought I would see if I could get ahold of her to see what she remembered. I went on Facebook to see what I could find and I could find her son, but not her. Although I remembered that I had fired her son thirty-something years ago I thought "what the hell, nobody can hold a grudge for that long, I certainly can't." So I FB messaged him and asked how I could get in touch with his mother. Sure enough he messaged me right back with her phone number. I called her and we made small talk for a while before I asked if she could remember the different family members she had worked with and if she had any recollections of those days that could help me with my book. She remembered that shortly after being hired she thought her mother could be a big help because most of the cleaning staff was too young and maybe her mother could go behind after them and fine tune each room. She also remembered that her son Tommy had worked for us for a short time and though there weren't any other actual relatives of hers that she had hired a few close friends. She struggled a little at that point and said she would have to ask Kathleen for more details.

"Better you than me," I commented back. "Kathleen still doesn't like me very much."

"I'm not sure I do either," Margarita shot back. "In fact when Tommy told me you might be calling I told him I might just give you a piece of my mind."

"Oh — wow," I hesitated. I only had recollections of Margarita as being a sweet smiling presence at the Inn.

"Yeah," she continued. "You were a little shit back then. Have you grown up at all?"

"I'm 62 years old," I laughed. "What was the problem?"

"Oh, you came back from college and you thought you knew it all, you didn't know shit. You tried to change everything that we were doing with all your forms and papers and you didn't know how to do anything. We were already doing it and all you had was your daddy and your college. I scrubbed toilets all over this valley and I had never been treated like that!"

"Crap," I was still laughing because that was thirty years ago and not only can I not hold onto anybody else's anger for that long I can't even hold onto my own! "I thought you would think I was a shit for being married and still harassing all the girls like I was single."

"That too," she was not about to give up her opportunity to give something back to someone she had obviously been angry with for a long time. "But no, it was how you came back after college and thought you knew it all. So, have you grown up at all? Did you ever have any children?"

"Margarita, that was 30 years ago. I lost a marriage over some of that stuff, I did a bunch of years of therapy, I've now been with the same woman now for 20 years and I have three kids and a granddaughter. Yeah, we were all stupid kids back then, me included."

"OK, well, just so you know how I feel," she seemed to calm down a bit and actually had a little giggle to her voice. "Maybe I could talk to Kathleen and see if she remembers anything useful."

That was how this tirade started so I figured I would let it rest at that point. "That would be great." I waited a few heartbeats. "So, do you have any stories from those days? You know, something that would add a little life to my story?"

"Well, the boob marks are something I will never forget."

"Boob marks?" I asked, instantly interested (I'll never grow up *that* much).

"Yeah," she went on without hesitation. "Rooms 17 and 19 had French doors," as if that would explain it. When she got nothing but silence from my side of the phone she continued, "There was nothing but a balcony and then vineyards out from those rooms. It seemed like two or three times a week we would find these twin smudge marks on the glass doors, maybe some elbow marks too." I was laughing and stunned at the same time. Why had I never heard about this in all the years at the Inn? "The crazy part is that we had to have two girls cleaning the glass, one on the inside and one on the outside because we never knew what side they were going to be on!"

(Innkeeper's note: Unfortunately those rooms now have cottages below them, so I am guessing this is no longer as common an occurrence).

We talked a while longer, both laughing and, hopefully, enjoying some cathartic moments, but Frank, her husband, had arrived home to take her to her doctor's appointment so we hung up. It's a small town and I learned long ago that holding onto stuff that happened more than even five years ago is pretty counterproductive. I'm hoping Margarita and maybe Kathleen can come to the same conclusion.

My former wife Nita had two younger sisters, Sheila and Jill, and as soon as they became hiring age they were on the payroll as well, working in, as I remember it, pretty much every department at one point or another. They were both excellent workers, Jill very bubbly and outgoing, Sheila more reserved and serious. Nita's mother Ruth also played a part. She is a tremendous artist — mostly in watercolors and mostly of local barns or broken down farm equipment — and a number of her pieces still hang around the Inn. In fact just a year or so ago my daughter Kelly (Ruth's granddaughter) redecorated a handful of rooms and brought in a few more of Ruth's paintings. Like Kathleen, Sheila had gotten some really good business and bookkeeping experience at the Inn and went on to work in accounting at various firms.

Alejandra Reyes was my Head Housekeeper shortly after Margarita. She also came with a good deal of family. Her daughter Lisa started working for us and I don't remember if she met Robert (her future live-in boyfriend and baby-daddy) on the job or if she brought Robert to us, but he soon became our handyman. Alejandra was a tough broad with a heart of gold. She ran a tight ship, made sure everyone put in a good hard day of work while at the same time looking out for all of those around her. She hired Marilena, Diana and Emma, all kinda

sorta related (nieces of her husband's from a previous marriage). Alejandra is now living in Idaho as is her daughter Lisa and Marilena. Maybe a little gun-shy, I found Alejandra's phone number and gave her a call. What a different reception! She was enthusiastically thrilled to hear from me and we talked for a long while about the good old days, all the parties I used to throw for the staff, the ski/gambling trips I used to take everyone on, and she promised to send me lots of photos she had stashed away in boxes.

Here' a little story about this wonderful family. I don't remember what year it was, but it was probably in the 80s when the week right around Christmas saw temperatures drop into the teens at night and barely got above freezing for a number of days in a row. Christmas Eve came along and the forecast was that it was going to drop into the single digits. Fortunately we do not have much of a Christmas business (read nothing at all) so a few years prior we had started a tradition of closing for

Christmas and giving the entire staff that holiday off, since we all pretty much work every other holiday.

However, this particular Christmas Robert had stashed some of his Christmas presents at the Inn so his girlfriend Lisa wouldn't find them at home. On Christmas morning he braved the record-breaking cold and snuck over to the Inn before his girlfriend woke up. He unlocked the front door to find it raining in the Common Room, the ceiling sheet rock sagging and the hardwood floors buckling. He surmised quickly that it had been raining for quite some time. Obviously I got a panicked call to come up right away. A few of the pipes in the attic had burst and — well — we had quite a mess on our hands. By the time I got there Robert had shut off the water to the entire building and the rain had turned from a deluge to a gentle patter. Merry F'n Christmas!

We were supposed to open on the 26th and we had a little bit of an issue! The presents Robert had showed up to retrieve now on the back burner he called his Lisa who worked the front desk and she called her mother Alejandra (who brought her husband along) and we all started trying to salvage what we could. I got Lisa on the phones and she started calling other hotels in the area to see where we could house fifteen couples while Ale started drying some of the precious antiques that filled the Common Room. As soon as the first pieces were dried we started hauling them into vacant rooms that had not been affected by the deluge. After a few hours we had cleared that piece of the disaster so we went upstairs to see what would greet us there. We found that the three guest rooms above the Common Room were in even worse shape. Here the ceilings had completely caved in with the sheetrock covering the furniture and carpets like a wet blanket and the offending busted pipes lurking above laughing at our flashlights. Furniture was still our first priority so we piled the sheetrock three feet high into the bathrooms to uncover beds and chairs and tables and as Robert and I started chucking sopping mattresses into the parking lot Ale started cleaning and drying more furniture. By the time we were done with that section it was getting dark and since we had also shut the electricity off to the building it was time to go home.

Fortunately we always close for the first few weeks of January so the list of guests we needed to call was not as long as it could have been. In our 40 years this still stands out as our biggest disaster and also the biggest display of a group effort to put everything into the common good of the business and to ignore what everyone would rather have been doing that particular day. Believe it or not we were reopened by mid-January and our insurance company actually came through and covered most all of our losses (not my normal experience with insurance companies).

By far the longest dynasty of family involvement in the Inn was the De Filipi/ Steelman family. I hired Diane De Filipi in 1988 as my first employee with the title of General Manager and she was with me through some of those tumultuous years of divorce and child-custody battles as well as a number of years when I was

single and ultimately she was my 'best woman' in my marriage to Lorinda. She was and still is a fast friend. Soon after Diane came on board her daughter and son-in-law moved north from Southern California. Soon her son-in-law Maury, a very talented gardener, was on our outside crew and a few months later her daughter Deniese was pulling evening desk shifts while pregnant with their first child, Kristen.

Though Diane came from a corporate background she is a natural-born innkeeper, with a quick wit and even quicker smile. Along with that came a fairly strong aversion to paperwork and filing which any good innkeeper shares. Who wants to be tied to a desk and filing cabinet when we can be out socializing with the guests? I guess I should take it as a compliment that the only reason Diane left the Inn was that after five years she had saved enough to buy her own inn, The Ink House just south of St. Helena. She now has pretty much the best career ever; she organizes and leads culinary tours of Italy and France. I had lunch with Diane just recently to see if she could add some color to her tenure at the Inn and boy could she. Immediately upon being seated at Farmstead we were in tears of laughter, recounting those days and all the crazy stories I had either forgotten or she had been two embarrassed to tell me before we had gotten to know each other well enough. After a couple stories she summed up her first few months at the Inn by naming them "Initiation by Naked,"

Just a couple weeks after being hired Diane was at the front desk by herself when a man walked around the corner. He had one piece of newspaper covering his junk and another behind, covering his trunk. Diane about jumped out of her skin.

"I'm so sorry," he stammered, obviously pained with embarrassment and fear that someone else might walk in at any moment. He could also no doubt see the horrification on Diane's face as she tried to avoid the natural tendency for her eyes to drift to the unusual aspect of this scene. "I was sitting on the deck reading my paper when the door slammed behind me," he explained sheepishly. "I'm locked out. I need a key to 26," he explained, his head jerking and peering

around to make sure they were still alone. Fumbling, Diane immediately went for the key drawer, pulled out a key to 26 (she was trained she was supposed to ask for ID if she didn't recognize the guest but …) and held it out to him.

"Ah," his eyes roving in desperation. He didn't have a free hand. They both quickly problem-solved and as he raised his elbow Diane, as best she could with her eyes averted, stuck the key in the man's armpit. Room 26 happened to be the furthest room from the office, all the way across the property and after he had been gone for a minute or two Diane realized she could have gone to the cabinet around the desk and gotten him a pool towel but it was now too late for that!

Literally a couple weeks later Diane was again working the desk alone when she got a phone call from Room 9 on the top floor of the Main Building. The guests informed Diane that someone was yelling from one of the other balconies that they were locked out and needed help. Master key in hand Diane rushed upstairs and started knocking on doors. She knocked on and entered three rooms before she found the right one. Immediately upon knocking on the door she could hear the guests inside yelling for help. She unlocked the door and rushed into the room only to come up short at the sight. The guests were frantically waving her forward, apparently quite chilled from being outside much longer than they had planned. They were completely naked and completely unconcerned about anything but getting back inside. Personally I think I would have just rushed to the door and let them in, but Diane is maybe a little shyer than I. Instead she told me that she grabbed the comforter off the bed, held it up between the guests and herself, made it blindly to the door and let them in, holding the quilt between them until they grabbed it and she made a hasty retreat.

Number three came right on the heels of number two. She was working the phones when she got a call from our good neighbor Russ (the father of two wonderful women who have worked for us over the years, Lizzy still does). Both laughing and a little alarmed Russ informed her that we had a guest on the roof of the Main Building — a three-story building with a steeply pitched

roof — frantically waving, and you guessed it — buck-naked. ON THE ROOF!

Well, Diane had had enough at this point. She stomped out the front door to where her son-in-law was planting the front entryway with blasting spring colors and demanded he go deal with this. WHAT KIND OF PLACE IS THIS she was wondering? Extremely reluctantly (I'm sure with the added pressure of the mother-in-law intimidation) Maury fetched a ladder, took it up to the third-floor fire escape landing and helped this guy down.

Innkeeper's note: I'm sure you are all wondering why or how all these patio and balcony doors can be so prone to locking people out of their rooms. I can tell you that there were a number of design issues with the various doors, but all of them have either been replaced or retrofitted to make these problems virtually impossible to replicate now. That by no means says that we haven't continued to have naked guest stories (there was one just a couple months ago where the guy tried to sneak out to his car to get something in the middle of the night and his wife fell so soundly asleep that he could not rouse her to let him back in) but at least the ones that were blatantly due to poor design by the Inn have been eliminated.

Of course there are the European women (or sure enough the American women who put on a fake French accent when approached) who just don't understand that topless is just not how we swing here. Early on, however, since we put in a pool I have felt that these situations take a certain amount of diplomatic authority that only the owner or Innkeeper possesses. Certainly these women should not be shamed or in any way made to feel judged or uncomfortable so Diane has thankfully never had to deal with any of these problems. There are standing orders among the staff to call the Innkeeper when these situations arise. Even if he is working from home or out to lunch, he is to be called and the women are not to be molested until he can handle it.

After a few failed attempts at finding a replacement for Diane I promoted Diane's daughter Deniese to the position of Manager. At this point her husband Maury was our Facilities Manager and this started the Steelman dynasty. Deniese is a wonderful woman and though she recently left the Inn after 23 years of service she is still a close friend and a frequent visitor to the Inn AND the most missed member of my staff by the guests. If I am on a hugging basis with a hundred of our guests Deniese is on a hugging basis with a thousand. That might be a slight exaggeration, but not much. Deniese's presence at the Front Desk, on the phone and with the staff was a huge factor in creating this wonderful place of comfort and casually friendly service. Maury prefers to stay out of the limelight and goes about keeping the Inn in tiptop shape without any of the hoopla. Maury has now been with us for 24 years and frankly we would all be completely lost without him.

We have 3 ¼ acres, ten buildings, 40 or so air conditioning systems, our own community water system, complete with two wells, various tanks and pressure pumps, gasoline generator for electrical back-up, filtration, softening and more, a whole communal sewer company with a few of our neighbors (the St. Helena Integrated Treatment Company, you can do the acronym), separate paint colors for every room, unique old furniture everywhere — and that's just the maintenance side. Then we have landscape gardens, culinary gardens and, until recently, a flock of 125 chickens laying eggs for our breakfast.

Maury gets to interface with the Health Inspector, the Fire Inspector, a staff of three or four, the neighbors (not always friendly) and — well — just about everyone who isn't a guest. I can guarantee you I would not be writing this book without Maury watching over things like he does. Both of Deniese and Maury's children have worked at the Inn, daughter Kristin at the Front Desk and son Daniel on all sorts of outside and special kitchen projects. They are both great kids (well, not really kids anymore) and have also added their own threads to the tapestry that is the Inn.

Deniese insists her first few years at the Inn were filled with ghosts. She came to the Inn about two years after my father passed away so she never met him, but she had heard stories that Ned was a bit of a prankster and is quite convinced to this day that Ned carried on those traditions for many years to follow. Since I

don't believe in such things (even though I have also witnessed things around the Inn that cannot be explained) I have always poo-pooed not only Deniese's stories but her regular insistence on having these stories a part of the training of any new desk clerk, especially if they were hired to work nights. The lore includes: open cabinets that were absolutely closed a moment before, footfalls in overhead rooms that are not occupied, doors that are strangely open, especially since they were locked with a key that no one on staff has except me. Things like that. And, certainly, Deniese points to her mother's experiences. "How could so many naked people get locked out of rooms? You think Ned wouldn't get a kick out of that?"

»———————————«

At the beginning of this chapter I gave a shout-out to my parents and my siblings, detailing their involvement with the Inn over the years, but I haven't mentioned my two older kids (third generation), Mike and Kelly who were involved and in Kelly's case is involved again. Mike worked at the Inn on the Front Desk through high school and a good deal of his college days. He definitely caught the hospitality bug, but probably smartly has decided to spread his wings in the world of large corporate hotels. After graduating from San Francisco State University with a degree in Hospitality Management Mike has gotten married and worked in a number of San Francisco hotels with a promotion each time he switches jobs. Since I have been at the same hotel, in the same job for 40 years I sat down with Mike recently to determine his intentions. The way I saw it he hadn't been at any one job for more than 6 to 9 months. He had now been at his current job for about 6 months so I was seeing the writing on the wall.

"So Mike," I started the delicate subject. "Do you like your current job?"

"Sure," Mike responded, digging into his half-pound burger.

"Gonna stay there for a while ('this time' was not spoken but implied)," I continued casually.

"Sure," Mike responded through a mouthful of burger. He chewed for a while, threw in a couple more fries. I had

Mike with wife Kristen

told him when I came down to visit he should pick a restaurant he had always wanted to go to but hadn't yet. Thinking he would pick something fancy I had dressed up a bit. He and his wife Kristen had shown up in shorts and flip-flops. When I asked him what was up Mike lamented how he had to wear a suit and tie to work every day and if I wanted to give him a special treat, a fancy restaurant was not the way to go about it.

Anyway, he kept chewing, maybe thinking, maybe wondering how to coin his comments. Finally he finished his thought, "At least another 9 months." I just about spewed *my* burger across the table. If a trusted employee of mine had given me that answer I would not have taken it well at all. Most of my staff have been with me for a dozen or more years and if they last less than two years I am quite disappointed. "If it's any more than that I will have gotten passed over," he explained, getting a little defensive. "My company is buying up hotels at a rate of about one every three months. They're already talking to me about my next move."

"What would be your next move?" now I was a bit intrigued.

"General Manager," he had stopped eating to give his announcement proper merit. "Probably something with 200 or 300 rooms."

"Oh," I said, my burger now tasting a little more like pie, humble pie. "Cool."

Kelly also worked the Front Desk through high school and some of college. A few years ago, while she was still in college she gave me a call. I could tell by her tone that this was a serious call so I stopped what I was doing and gave her my attention.

"Dad, could I come back to the Inn and take over your job?" she just came out with. "Don't you want to start slowing down a bit?"

You think I was floored with Mike's announcement that he was only planning on being at his job for another 9 months, this little question just about dropped me *through* the floor.

"Wha??" was about all I could get out.

But Kelly was prepared. "I know I can't just take over like that! You'd have to do some training!"

"Ya think?!!" I was startled to understand that I was going to have to actually respond, that she thought she had seriously thought this through. "I guess I should take it as a compliment that I make it look so easy, but I've been doing this for a long time. It's not something I just teach you! It's years of making contacts and making friends. It's who to call for what and how to treat people. It's juggling a million details every day and making it look like everything is completely under control." But then it occurred to me this phone call had to be about something else completely. "So, what's up?"

"I just want to come back and work at the Inn," she explained.

"You're in the middle of a semester," I was confused but the warning bells were going off.

"Well, that's the deal," her voice got a little smaller. "You know I was sick for those couple of weeks and I got too far behind ..."

"And," I was going to make her say it.

"And I dropped out," she finally spilled.

"Well, you're right about one thing," my anger apparent. "You're going to have to find a job. I'll start helping you out again when you're re-enrolled." Obviously the call went on for a while longer but I made it clear she couldn't come back to the Inn under these circumstances and she wasn't going to get any further financial support until she was back in school.

Seven years later I couldn't be more pleased. Kelly finished her degree in Interior Design, got married to a great guy, produced an amazing granddaughter and has been welcomed back to the

Kelly, Fiona and Matt

Inn with open arms. She is indeed now being tutored by the old man, working her tail off and making it look easy to those around her.

Here is a little story about how Kelly can stay calm under pressure. Just a few months ago I was at my weekly poker game when I got a frantic call from the Inn. "The Inn's on fire, get here now!" Click.

Adrenaline dumped into my system and I was out the door leaving my friends

at the table bewildered and concerned. I have had other emergencies in my life where a few miles seemed like a hundred, but the three miles to the hotel in my company car (it's a quick little thing) normally a the five-minute drive didn't really take all that long. By the time I got to the end of the driveway there were four fire trucks on Lodi Lane waiting as back-up and four more trucks up the driveway pulling hoses and evacuating guests. Since for years I threw an annual dinner party for our local volunteer Fire Department I am well known by all of them and they waved me through their phalanx as I drove in. I parked and ran to the front entrance, but my daughter Kelly and Cory, an out-of-town contractor I had hired to do a bunch of ADA improvements, were out front collecting their nerves. Cory had spent the night in one of the rooms instead of making the two-hour drive home just to turn around and come back in the morning.

"It's out, it's out," was the first thing I heard as I approached. Both were visibly shaken but not injured so I turned to go back to my poker game. Huh?

"What happened, is everything alright?" I asked as I got close enough.

"We got it out just in time," Cory explained. "They were just hooking up their hoses when I rushed out to tell them it was out. The kitchen is a mess, but if they had gotten their hoses going it would have been a lot worse."

Since I wasn't there, here is my daughter's version (she was living right across the street from the Inn at the time):

It was about 9 p.m. and I had just gotten Fiona (my amazing granddaughter) down when I got a frantic call from Jackie that the Inn was on fire. I flew out of the house and up the driveway and by the time I got to the front door there was heavy black smoke pouring out the door. Jackie was out front distraught. "It's in the kitchen, I called the fire department and Jim, but I don't know what else to do!" she was able to get out.

"Go around to the side entrance and make sure all the guests are getting out," I yelled as I rushed inside. The smoke was so thick I couldn't breathe until I realized if I got low enough I could at least get a little air. I made my way into the kitchen and could see the stove was blazing up to the ceiling. I was out of breath at that point so I headed back outside. Taking as many deep breaths as possible I headed back in. I knew there was a fire extinguisher on the wall so I grabbed it and started spraying the stovetop. Glasses were exploding and the fire seemed to be growing.

Just then the phone rang and I thought it might be the Fire Department so I answered it, "Good evening, The Wine Country Inn, this is Kelly?"

"This is Liz, I hear the Inn is on fire," our next door neighbor and employee was calling after she heard the alert on her police scanner.

"I can't talk right now," I screamed. "The Inn's on fire!!" and hung up.

I kept at the fire with the extinguisher and kept running outside to breathe. On about my third trip Cory came running up after being alerted by Jackie and as I took my next trip back into the kitchen Cory ran to turn off the gas and electricity. As soon as the gas was shut off I could see the flames recede and with the last few shots left in the extinguisher

we got it out. I headed back outside and realized the fire department had arrived and were quickly unrolling and hooking up their hoses.

"Wait, wait, wait," I yelled. "I think we got it."

Obviously the fire crew came in and checked everything thoroughly, but the fire was out and they didn't need to hose anything down.

I guess the amazing part of this chapter is that we don't have any earthquake stories. I am imagining many of the people reading this book live outside of California and the main rap on California from non-Californians seems to be that they would never live here because of all the earthquakes. And that is fine, because we really don't need any more people actually living here — coming for a quick visit and then returning home is great, but living here …? Anyway, the Inn has stood for 40 years and has definitely rocked and rolled a few times over those years but we have never sustained any damage besides, literally, maybe one or two knick-knacks falling over, but truthfully I can't even remember if that

Oops, looks like Fiona jumped between Alura and Lorinda

they hear the story of all the family connections. And though the "Ma" part of my life is certainly an enormous support to everything I do, she does not work with me at the Inn. My wife Lorinda is the Operating Room Manager at our local St. Helena Hospital, working her own crazy hours and running her own eclectic crew. It's hard to believe that it has been nearly 20 years since she crooked her finger at me, inviting me to explain how she knew me while enjoying the music at an OGIM (Oh Gosh It's Monday) concert at Domaine Chandon Winery. Fortunately I had already spotted this beauty in the crowd and had asked a friend if he knew her. My friend Al had reminded me that the reason I knew her was because my best friend Jeff had dated her for a short while the year before, so when Lorinda crooked her finger at me across the crowd (it was the third pass I had made in front of her trying to get her attention) I was

has happened. However, the last one on August 24, 2014, affected a great number of our staff who live in Napa just 20 miles south who lost pretty much everything breakable in their homes, causing them great stress and loss, and I don't want to make light of that. The Inn and the upper Napa Valley in general has been saved from any significant amount of damage in the 50 years I have lived here.

》———《

Most people assume that the Inn is a "Ma & Pa" business, especially when ready to speak with authority about our connection. We danced the rest of that evening and since this concert series ran every Monday through the month of June by the time OGIM was over for the year we were pretty much inseparable. Fortunately, however, inseparable did not translate to work.

We both love what we do, but we also love being able to come home and not talk shop. We lament and we vent and we commiserate about circumstances and events that are at least one step removed from the other's realities, and that is a very good thing. Our daughter Alura is currently in 7th grade and has a very full life without needing to follow Daddy to work. Between dance, yoga, way more homework than I can ever remember having and what appear to be perpetual sleepovers with girlfriends, when would she find time to help me out at the Inn? Though that's not exactly true. Many evenings Alura babysits her niece, Fiona, (just nine years younger than she is) which allows my other daughter Kelly to put in the hours needed for me to take some time off (maybe finish a book or two). So

I guess it all stays in the family one way or another.

And then there are Tracy and Guy, the dynamic kitchen duo. Tracy, who still drives for our Inn-Cursions (a day-tour service to the local wineries) started as our breakfast cook over fifteen years ago. I think she had been with me for a few years ago when she approached me with the idea of hiring her younger brother Guy who had spent 25 years in the sanitation industry but who had a degree in Hospitality from my own alma mater San Francisco City College (at that point the best two-year Hospitality program I was able to find). I met Guy and chatted with him for a while and knew immediately he would fit in. I have a million stories about these two, but I still see them almost every day so I guess I have to be careful. My favorite story, though, is Guy's immediate rise to fame. I hired Guy as his sister's prep cook and within a month or so he had promoted himself to chef. And I mean promoted himself, as in going out to the guests and the local wineries and anyone who would listen and promoting the Inn, promoting the Inn's food, promoting all the wineries that were quickly becoming his friends and promoting the idea that the Inn was classy enough to have a chef. This level of marketing sophistication (read self-promotion) had literally never occurred to me. Though I was very proud of the breakfast we served and we were developing a very nice evening food program for our nightly wine tasting our food was, and mostly still is, a collection of home-cooking family recipes, simple recipes that did not rise to the level Chefdom. But Chef Guy had no

Tracy & Guy

such conflicts. His promotional mindset fit perfectly with the new national trend to raise chefs around the country to Rock-Star status and we might as well ride those coattails. But what of his sister Tracy? She was a little more old-school and just wasn't comfortable with the hooty-tooty title of Chef, so when I was reprinting Guy's business cards I asked Tracy, still Guy's direct supervisor, what title she wanted. All was settled when she chose Kitchen Goddess. Though Guy retired a few years ago Tracy still drives for our day tour service we call Inn-Cursions. She is celebrating her fifteenth year with us.

I put this recipe under Guy's story because he loved to make this dish along with the joke, "I need to take my cholesterol pills just to make this recipe." But that is not why I loved it. This recipe was first introduced by Diane on one of our infamous ski/gambling trips I used to take the whole staff on. These trip were famous for trying out new breakfast recipes and Diane had gotten up early to put this together before a bunch of us hit the slopes (the gamblers missed out because they didn't usually get up until lunch). I will never forget that after a big square of this filling egg dish I skied for six hours straight and drove home never even thinking about lunch. When I got home I was blown away. I NEVER forget lunch and couldn't imagine I had after skiing all day!

The last family grouping we currently have running are the Llamas sisters. Though at one point there were three Llamas sisters on the payroll: Yolanda, my Head Housekeeper, Rosie, Kitchen Assistant and Maria, also in the kitchen, Maria is no longer at the Inn. Yolanda has been with us for 19 years now and Rosie for 17, and both are integral members of the staff.

I also need to also give a shout-out to a bunch of other family teams that maybe didn't have the longevity or the multigenerational aspects to their involvements, but life would not have been the same without: the Stevenson sisters (and Richard), the Milat sisters, Michael and Susan, Jill and Deniese (they were like sisters).

Grilled Bread

by Jim

INGREDIENTS

Good Bread

Some sort of fat, butter, olive oil, bacon grease?

Your imagination

I guess I have to ask, who invented the toaster — and why? I'm guessing it was one of those Christmas gadgets like the crock-pot, the mandolin slicer or one of those little hand blenders, all of which I have stashed in some drawer or cabinet somewhere in my kitchen. And every one of them I drag out once or twice a year just to justify holding onto it and not dumping it in the yard sale box. But the toaster really caught on, so much so that most of us have given it special — maybe even necessary status as one of those only appliances that deserve permanent counter space. But why? What does it do? It does a rather mediocre job of browning slices of bread (usually too thinly sliced bread to my taste) in a reasonably short period of time with little fuss or muss.

If you're toasting a slice of Wonder — well, just go ahead. But if you've got a decent slice of sourdough or a multi-grain something or other, or better yet a bagel (English muffins are a little challenging) and you take that same butter, you melt it in a pan and grill that same bread over medium heat for maybe a minute longer than the toaster is going to take, now you have a breakfast delight that lives in a whole different nation than that little semi-dried hunk of gluten you could have put in the toaster. But that's just the beginning! Experiment with a little extra virgin olive oil instead of the butter (I think this usually needs a little salt, too). It has a completely different flavor and might be a little much for some for breakfast, but it will definitely get you thinking about fixing some spaghetti for dinner. Now imagine taking that garlic butter that lives in your fridge and frying up a thicker slice of really good French bread. If you're like me that bread is no longer an after-thought side dish to the meal, it becomes the inspiration for new creations, like Adult Grilled Cheese. Don't you have at least a few unusual cheeses living in your cheese drawer from your last party? A grilled breakfast sandwich with a couple slices of ham, a fried or scrambled egg and some hearty mustard? Who needs a Panini press to make a Panini? Just another gadget taking up space in my already crowed kitchen. Use another heavy skillet on top and by the time you brown both sides it will take you about as long as it would to find your press and pull it out of the cabinet. Do I need to say it again? Grilled bread rocks so much harder than toast.

Death by Cheese
by Diane

INGREDIENTS

12 eggs

1 cup flour

2 tsp baking powder

8 oz cream cheese, cut into cubes and floured to keep from sticking together

2 lbs jack cheese, cut into cubes and floured to keep from sticking together

¼ tsp salt

2 cups milk

16 oz cottage cheese

4 tbls butter

DIRECTIONS

1. Preheat oven to 325 degrees.

2. Cut cream cheese and jack cheese into 1" cubes. Use some of the 1 cup of flours to pour over and mix with cheeses to keep from sticking together.

3. Beat eggs in a large bowl. Add remaining flour, baking powder, salt and milk. Use whip to make sure all flour is absorbed. Whisk in cottage cheese. Stir in cubed cheese and any flour that remains on cutting board.

4. Pour into large greased baking dish. Dot the top evenly with the butter.

5. Bake for approximately 45 minutes until puffed and golden brown on top. Allow to cool for 10 minutes before serving.

Wine Country Inn Granola
by Sheila

INGREDIENTS

2 cups Quaker old fashion oats

1 cup almonds, slivered
(preferred) or sliced

¼ cup brown sugar

¼ cup butter

1 cup coconut, flaked

Sprinkle of cinnamon and salt

¼ cup honey

1 cup raisins

DIRECTIONS

1. Mix together oats and almonds across a large baking pan.

2. In a small bowl stir together melted butter and honey (it helps if the butter is still warm). Pour mixture over oats and almonds, mix well and spread evenly across the pan. Sprinkle with the brown sugar, cinnamon and salt over the coated oats and almonds mix lightly.

3. Bake at 350 degrees until golden brown, stirring regularly. Then add coconut and bake until medium brown, still stirring often.

4. Remove from the oven and add raisins. Stir frequently while cooling to keep from sticking together.

5. Store in an air tight container for up to a month (though the granola you eat at the Inn was probably made yesterday).

Sourdough Eggs
by Diane

INGREDIENTS

Serves 4

6 slices extra sourdough bread

2 cups grated cheddar cheese

5 eggs

½ tsp salt

1 ½ heaping tbls spicy or
Dejon mustard

½ cup thinly sliced mushrooms

2 cups milk

½ medium onion, diced
pretty small

¼ tsp fresh ground pepper

DIRECTIONS:

Prepare the night before

1. Cut bread into small cubes. Place ½ of bread cubes into a 9 x 9 oil-coated baking dish.

2. Sprinkle with two cups cheese, onion and mushrooms. Add a second layer of bread and top with remaining cheese. Beat eggs, milk, mustard, salt and pepper together. Pour this mixture evenly over the casserole.

3. Cover with foil and refrigerate overnight.

4. Next morning bake at 325 degrees for approximately 50 minutes until the top is golden and lightly crusted.

This is a recipe I have a lot of fun with at home. It's a great way to use cheeses leftover from a party or some of that Costco size cheese that might be getting a little funky. I have also been known to add some hot sauce to the egg mixture or substitute canned Anaheim chilies for the mushrooms. And of course some crumbled up bacon, caramelized onions (in addition to or instead of the raw) roasted garlic, leftover ham or sausage, none of that can hurt!

Huevos Francasis

INGREDIENTS

Serves 4

8 eggs

4 sweet French bread
   sandwich rolls

2 tlbs butter

4 tbls red salsa

4 tbls green salsa

½ lb cheddar cheese, shredded

½ lb jack cheese, shredded

½ cup sour cream

DIRECTIONS

1. Heat an inch or so of poaching water in a large skillet. Slice almost completely open and butter all rolls.

2. Place rolls on a cookie sheet and place them under the broiler and toast lightly. Just before coming to a boil, carefully break all eggs into water to poach the eggs. After eggs are firmly poached ladle one egg on each side of the sandwich rolls with a slotted spoon.

3. Dollop a large spoonful of red salsa on one of the eggs on each roll and a spoonful of green salsa on the other egg.

4. Cover all four sandwich rolls with a generous portion of the two cheeses. Place rolls back under broiler and broil until cheese is bubbling and browned.

5. Serve immediately with a dollop of sour cream over each egg.

"Sugar Pie" Pumpkin Pie
by Deniese

INGREDIENTS

2 eggs

2 cups "sugar pie" fresh pumpkin

¾ cup sugar

½ tsp salt

1 tsp cinnamon, ground

½ tsp ginger, ground

¼ tsp cloves, ground

1 2/3 cups evaporated milk

2 homemade or store-bought 9"
   pie crusts

DIRECTIONS

1. Cut up "sugar pie" pumpkin and remove skin. Boil pumpkin in salted water for 20 minutes or until soft. Drain well, mash and set aside to cool.

2. After cool, add all other ingredients and mix well. Pour into pie crusts and bake at 425 degrees for 15 minutes.

3. Reduce heat to 350 and bake for 45 minutes.

4. Let cool for at least a half hour and then chill in the refrigerator for at least one hour before serving. Top with piles of whipped cream.

Personally after any kind of feast this pie is usually served with a much prefer my pie the next morning with the whipped cream in my coffee. Is that just me?

CHAPTER 7

Guests Who Became Family

Though I am on a hugging basis with a hundred or so of our return guests, a few stand out as family. The Arutes have been coming to the Inn three to five times a year for at least 25 years. They live in the foothills of the Sierra Nevadas, a bit east of Sacramento. They have a group of friends who also enjoy the Inn and this group makes a pilgrimage to the Inn every fall, booking their rooms before they leave for the next year. They are special people and I will tell you a little story about their impact on the Inn. Back in the early 90s I was in a management meeting with my senior staff reporting on a large research project I had just completed. Our occupancy had dipped from a recent recession and though the economy was recovering our occupancy seemed to be lagging behind. I had set out to find out why, and after a month or more of canvassing other hotels in the area by making dozens of phone calls to each as a potential guest (this was before you could just go on-line to gather all this information in a matter of hours) I figured out that my competition was filling up better than we were and at a higher rate! This was not OK with me, especially since one of those was a Best Western and others did not offer the amenities we did. The surprising conclusion I had come to was that our rates were too low; that we could improve our occupancy by raising our rates, and not by a little bit, but by a lot! I was explaining to my management team that my conclusions were that on a list of Napa Valley lodging people must be assuming that there must be something wrong with our property if our rates are so low. My staff was skeptical to say the least. When I had finished my report there was dead silence. I was proposing a 20 percent increase in our rates at a time when our occupancy was slumping. But I think my staff could feel that I was committed to this line of thinking so my manager thought she might circumvent my head of steam and suggest, "But what about all of our old-time return guests? We're going to lose a bunch of them. What about the Arutes and the Fennels and the Teals and the Days?"

We went round and round until finally I asked, "How many folks are we really talking about?" When it got down to it there was a list of about thirty couples that had been coming for more than ten years and most of them came multiple times per year. I said, "Well hell, we can't make huge business decisions that are dictated by such a small piece of our business.

Why don't we just give those folks a huge lifetime discount off whatever rates we agree on and call it a day." And I know a lot of you aren't going to like the end of this story, but it turned out I was right and shortly after we raised our rates to be just a bit higher than our direct competition our occupancy immediately improved. I can see where **we** would call that a win/win but you might think of it as a bit of a bummer.

As this story goes, the Arutes and their friends continued their yearly pilgrimages to the Inn and were (and still are) very appreciative of their lifetime discounts. A number of years later I was expecting my third child in September of 2001. I was a very proud papa who would regale anyone who would listen about this upcoming birth and even though my wife has never worked at the Inn (she is the Operating Room Manager at our local St. Helena Hospital) I would show off pictures and tell stories of the pregnancy and all the work it had taken to get that job done! The Arutes got no shortage of these stories. Well, the normal date for their group's visit is in late September so when they arrived I

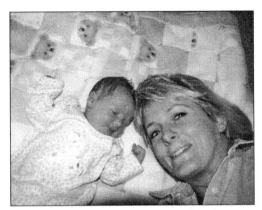
Baby Alura with mother Lorinda on the quilt made by the Arutes and friends.

was armed with an array of photos, a full rendition of the birth (including the twin towers tragedy during one of our false labors), a full description of a beautiful little girl and a complete report about the health of both mother and daughter, all the good stuff. But the Arutes and their friends had a little bundle of joy, too. After I had completed my self-indulgent rant of this perfectly wonderful event they presented me with a quilt the women of the group had gotten together to make for me in anticipation of the birth. I was (and still am) overwhelmed by this gesture. How wonderful a gift and how wonderful a thought that they would even think to do this.

Another story you might find fun, although it wasn't fun for our guests: A long-time return guest couple was getting a divorce. Apparently within the negotiations of this divorce the Wine Country Inn came up as a point of contention. This couple had been coming up for years on a particular weekend to attend a wine release party at one of the local wineries. They both wanted to keep coming up to the Inn and they both wanted to continue to attend this party, but neither wanted to see the other one there. We were blissfully unaware of 90 percent of this, except that when the gentleman of the now estranged couple called to make his reservation he told us to redo his guest history to include the new woman in his life instead of his former. We were saddened by this, but we also needed to prepare the staff. This is one problem we do not need to deal with very often, but for as close as we get to some of our guests this is something we need to flag and make sure our staff is made aware of on the day of arrival. The appointed date arrived and the staff was prepped. But not for what ended up happening. The estranged wife arrived first, with her new man. Apparently this new man had booked their room under his name after she had described the room she wanted, the room her and her husband had always stayed in. There was certainly nothing we could do at this point on a completely sold out weekend, but we also knew that he had not gotten it exactly right. But he had gotten it pretty darn close. He had booked the room right next door. Not knowing quite what to do we checked them into their assigned room (since all of our rooms are so different we can't just swap room assignments around like in a big hotel) and waited for the fireworks. The estranged husband arrived a couple hours later and at that point we had decided it was none of our business and that maybe they had worked this whole thing out between the four of them. Well, no, they hadn't. In fact both decided to leave for the winery party at exactly the same time and bumped into each other right outside their rooms. The estranged husband was horrified. Not only had his ex decided to show up, but they were now sharing a common wall (we have since retrofitted these walls, but at the time they were quite thin and who knows what kind of noise they had already been making!) Though we don't know what was said at this point we do know that there was enough heated emotion and awkwardness to make us all uncomfortable for the weekend. The happy ending to the story is that the estranged couple ended up working out at least some sort of a truce because, though they made sure they didn't book rooms right next to each other, both couples continued to come to the Inn for that weekend for at least a few years more. Now just one of the couples comes and things are a little calmer.

———————»————————«———————

Bill and Cheryl have been good friends of the Inn for more years than I can count. They are soft-spoken wonderful, dedicated guests who have stayed with us three or four times a year for at least the last twenty years. Molly was our "house cat" for almost that long. But Molly was starting to misbehave. We had gotten word for over a year that Molly had been sleeping around. Whoever got back to the Inn with the most enticing leftovers was Molly's new bedmate and even with the strict Inn policy that Molly was not to be tramping around — well — it seemed no one was listening. Now that's all cute and all, but Bill and Cheryl came up much too often to always go to the French Laundry or Terra or one of the other Michelin-Star quality eateries, and certainly didn't like getting snubbed by Molly. Additionally, Molly was putting on a few too many pounds. The rich lifestyle of the Napa Valley demands discipline if you are to remain healthy and Bill and Cheryl were just not around often enough, nor did they come home early enough to control this cat's appetites. Maybe they planned this, we'll never know, but one evening I was hosting our wine social and Molly snuck in the front door, tempted by the aromas of Chef Guy's evening creations. I'm sure it had been at least a couple hours since a guest had offered her a morsel or two of their lunch, or Molly had become so jaded by the Inn's cuisine. Either way, she launched herself onto the 150-year-old harvest table I was standing behind and started going at the salmon and green olive dip I had specifically requested. I could not react quickly enough. Horrified guests, including Bill and Cheryl, sitting quietly at a corner table, witnessed me grabbing Molly by the scruff of her neck and depositing her unceremoniously out the front door. Non-cat-lovers were horrified that a cat had been in the food, cat-lovers were horrified that I had treated my cat so roughly, while only Bill and Cheryl seemed — well — I don't know what they seemed, but the next morning they arrived at breakfast a little late, having driven thirty miles to the closest pet supply house to purchase a cat carrying case. Between my manager Deniese and themselves they had decided that Molly was going home with them to sunny Southern California. Thinking this was a dandy solution we said our good byes to Bill, Cheryl and Molly. Within a week we got an email from Cheryl with a link to a new website. Molly was now streaming video of her new home and though I am imagining she was not loving the new diet she had been placed on, she was probably loving the idea that she wouldn't have to be prowling the night, looking for love in all the wrong places.

The Wine Country Inn is indeed out in the country, surrounded on all sides by vineyards and on two of those sides by wineries as well. Both Freemark Abbey and Trinchero Family Estates have semi-wild cats that help keep the rodent populations down. Since we are close enough to each of them for spillover within a month of Molly's departure we had a bob-tailed little runt of a cat skulking around the property. We believe that both Molly and our new cat Bob were indeed the runts of some litters and had been forced to run for their lives. Being a runt myself until my mid-twenties and five nights a week of martial arts training, I could relate. So Bob was allowed to stay and within months Bob was putting Molly to shame when it came to sleeping around. He became a regular part of our check-in policy: "Bob is a wonderful outdoor cat and contrary to what he will say we feed him well. Please ignore his pitiful attempts at sympathy and keep him outside and let us feed him." Yeah, right! Cat lovers (of which I am not) have no self-control. Cat lovers miss their own cats even when separated for only a few days. Probably half of you reading this book know exactly what I am talking about. So Bob soon became fat and sassy. A sweet guy, he wrangled his way into many a bedchamber and many a leftover from the tables of some of the finest restaurants in the country. His picture popped up on our website and within a year guests were returning with their first question being, "Where's Bob?" Not, "How have you been, Jim," as I am giving them a hug. Not "It's so great to be back!" as we disengage and they look around at the new decorating my daughter had just completed, but rather, "Where's Bob?" That's all well and good, I guess. I don't get it, but at least they're coming back and more than happy to be doing so.

You guessed it, within a year Bob was losing his fine physique and though he was still quick to greet every guest returning from dinner he was lazing around

Bob the Cat

much too much to maintain a healthy lifestyle. And sure enough, after a few years of this decadent living he too started jumping up on the serving table during our social hour. On an off-chance they could help, Deniese called Bill and Cheryl. Two days later Bill and Cheryl showed up after driving nine hours from their home in Southern California with a cat-crate, spent one night (on us) and relocated Bob into retirement to his new home in the sun-belt. Bill and Cheryl still come up regularly with updates on Bob.

Steve and Carol have been staying with us for at least thirty years. For the first

twenty years I knew him as Bill, but about ten years back he corrected me, "My name is actually Steve and I would like you to start calling me by my real name."

Now, I am terrible with names, but I know this man well. We have sat over many a glass of wine, he has a condominium in Tahoe where both my staff and I have stayed on at least fifteen occasions and he has another condo on Maui that I have used a couple of times. I was floored that I could be such an absolute bone-head. "I've been calling you Bill for 15 years. What's the deal, how could you let me do that?"

Turns out he was kind of embarrassed. "It's not your fault," he finally said. "At the company I worked at for the last 20 years there was already a Steve Llorens, so to keep the confusion to a minimum I started going by my middle name, Bill. But I'm not with the company any more so I want to reclaim my real name."

Phew, I thought to myself, it wasn't me for once. So after a few stumbles Bill has become Steve and we have moved on. Unfortunately, Steve and Carol have moved on to Hawaii so they don't make it to the Inn nearly as often as they used to but when they do we still spend an hour or so catching up.

»———————«

George and Lisa are the only guests who have brought their daughter to stay with us for so long that she has now moved out and is living on her own. And where did she decide to live up until just recently? The Napa Valley! It definitely makes me feel old when things like this happen. I think Kristen was probably six or seven when she first stayed with us and now she has been living out on her own for more than a few years. How does that happen?

We are very glad to have George and Lisa stay with us. George is a retired California Highway Patrol Officer but I think at the time of this story he was still an active patrolman. They were checked-in to the Brandy Barn and were just returning from a day of touring when George noticed smoke coming from a room on the lower floor. He immediately sent Lisa to the room to alert the Front Desk while he went to investigate. The door to the room in question had been propped open so he immediately identified it as a laundry room. In the back by the dryers the room was fully engulfed in flames, now curling across the ceiling and reaching out into the rest of the room. Outside, strategically place for just such an occasion was a hand-held fire extinguisher. George pulled the pin and started hosing down the fire. He fought it valiantly until the extinguisher was empty but all he had been able to accomplish was to slow the spread. The base of the fire seemed to be behind the dryers and he couldn't quite direct the spray to the right angle. But he had done what was necessary because moments after the extinguisher had run dry Maury, my Facilities Manager, was pulling a watering hose from its cute little holder with the water at full-blast. Maury was able to arc his stream over the top of the dryers and flood behind them with water. Electrical breakers started popping at that point, but that was the least of their worries. As the source fire slowly died Maury went to work on the sheets and towels that had fallen victim to the flames, many of them smoldering deep into the stacks. Others from Maury's outside crew soon arrived and by the time the fire trucks rolled up the fire was successfully out, each stacked sheet and towel having been pulled from the shelves and thoroughly doused. So, thank you, George, for your quick thinking and I hope to hell we comped your stay for at least that stay. I can't imagine if we would have had to rebuild the entire Brandy Barn. As it was I don't think we had more than $20,000 worth of damage, which seems like an absolute bargain to me now.

Innkeeper's Note: make sure you clean behind your dryer on a regular basis (we now do it weekly). From what the fire department and the insurance company told me, lint fires are one of the most common kinds.

About ten days later, just up the road from the Inn, my family home caught fire in the middle of the night and we were not so lucky. My mother barely made it out alive and at least a third of our home burned to the ground, destroying tons of family heirlooms and memories. All I can say about that disaster is that if an insurance company says it is "on your side"

don't believe it. The astounding amount of crap they pulled to get out of paying for the loss was beyond comprehension. Masood at Greenspan Adjusters was a Godsend and after a year and a half we ended up getting a decent settlement but I never could have done it on my own.

Doug and Lois are an elegant couple. They usually stay with us either before or after Doug stays out at the Bohemian Grove, an enclave of rustic camps over in Monte Rio where who knows what goes on. The Bohemian Grove is a legendary icon of American power shrouded in mystery and myth where captains of industry, CEOs of Fortune 500 companies and an occasional United States President gather to "rough it" and do guy stuff. Monte Rio is indeed a rough little town about 40 miles west of the Inn, just a few miles from the California coast. It is heavily forested with thousand-year-old redwoods and equally old traditions. If you're interested, look it up on Wikipedia and you'll get a clue what kind of place this is, but you would never know from Doug and Lois. Well, except Doug came to me once, very quietly, and told me the hard-boiled eggs we had started including in our breakfast buffet were just too hard to peel. Really I thought to myself, a hard-boiled egg is just a hard-boiled egg (I didn't study these for my degree in culinary arts). But Doug is a good customer — a trusted customer — so I went into the kitchen, pulled an egg out of the refrigerator and started peeling it. He was right, it was almost impossible to get the shell off without taking half the white along with it. Wha? I tried another one, same thing. This was unacceptable. These were the finest eggs ever laid. We had our own flock of 125 chickens and these eggs were no more than a day old when they had been boiled and no more than a day old since then. I talked to Chef, I talked to the other kitchen staff, I talked to everyone except my manager Deniese or her husband Maury who, before moving to Napa Valley had worked for a dairy and egg distributer in Southern California. The mystery, and my frustration continued for a week or two (I'm not the kind of guy that just lets something like this slide). I

researched "boiling eggs" on-line and came up with a new technique: put the eggs in a pot of cold water, with at least an inch of water over the eggs, bring them to a boil (slowly if you are using a high BTU commercial stove), let them boil for one minute, then turn the heat off and let them steep in the nearly boiling water for 12 minutes, drain and cool. We instituted this cooking technique and the eggs turned out perfectly cooked, but the shells still completely adhered to the whites. Finally in desperation I happened to bring it up in a management meeting.

"Yeah," Deniese responded. "The eggs are too fresh." She just delivered her verdict like that, cold and flat, like it was obvious.

"What are you talking about," I demanded. Deniese and Maury just looked at each other like the rest of us were ignorant savages.

Maury was a little more understanding of our lack of knowledge. "Eggs need to be at least a week or so old before you can hard-boil them. It has something to do with a thin membrane between the white and the shell that slowly disengages from the shell as it ages. You've probably never noticed before because any egg you get from a store has been stored for at least a few weeks before you buy it, in unrefrigerated warehouses by the way. Eggs really don't need to be refrigerated for months if they're not cracked or cooked."

Wow, that was just wrong. Not that they turned out to be wrong, but that the answer was so simple and yet so bizarre. Within a few minutes we had a system worked out where we would hold a few eggs back from the eggs coming directly from the chickens and rotate them through an aging process so that the eggs Doug peeled in the morning had been aged for at least ten days. Doug was pleased next time he stayed, not only because he could now easily peel his eggs, but he was also pleased that he had been a part of improving something at the Inn.

There are a ton of other guests with tons of other stories but we can't tell them all. Here is a shout out to some of our other repeat guests who stand out in my mind. Just like the Oscars I'm sure I will forget some very important names, but here is my best effort. Thanks to: the Carsons, Seveys, Michaelses, Baileys, Masakises, Musnickises, Mederoses, Inces, Hildebrands, Shipleys, Rileys, Rosenbergs, Longs, Dubbinks and Al.

The Inn is known for its fun selections of dipping oils. In fact I just got a call from a friend who said her Meyer lemon tree is ready for harvest so I will be heading down to Napa to harvest these unique fruit later today. I will probably then stop by my favorite spice shop in the Oxbow market to see what new kinds of paprika they have and then head back to the Inn to whip up some super fresh recipe for tonight's guests.

Meyer Lemon with Smokey Paprika Dipping Oil
by Jim

INGREDIENTS

1 Meyer lemon, juice and zest

4 clove garlic, minced

½ cup young, green extra
    virgin olive oil

1 pinch of salt

1 large pinch of smoky paprika

1 oz freshly grated
    parmesan cheese

DIRECTIONS

1. Juice the lemon into a wide, shallow serving dish. Add minced garlic and let 'cook' for a few minutes.

2. Add the rest of the ingredients and mix so that salt and paprika are well absorbed and well distributed. The oil and juice will not be emulsified but that is fine.

3. Garnish with parmesan cheese.

If you prefer to have the juice and oil more emulsified, make this mixture (or any of the following recipes in a mason jar, add all ingredients and shake vigorously to incorporate and then pour into serving bowl. Serve with 1 inch squares of your favorite sourdough. Encourage your guests to dip the bread as opposed to spooning the oil over the bread. At the Inn we can't do this, but at home it is so much more fun to dip and swirl.

Balsamic & Fine Herb Dipping Oil

by Jim

INGREDIENTS

½ cup extra virgin olive oil

4 cloves garlic, minced

1 large pinch dried Italian fine herb mix

1 pinch sea salt

1 large pinch pepper flakes

A few large drizzles of the best Balsamic vinegar you can find

2 sprigs fresh rosemary

DIRECTIONS

1. Add all ingredients except vinegar and rosemary sprigs into a wide, shallow serving dish. Mix lightly until garlic, herbs and pepper flakes are incorporated. Let stand for an hour or more.

2. Just before serving drizzle Balsamic vinegar, letting it remain in little pockets. Add rosemary sprigs as garnish and serve with crusty squares of sourdough or rye.

The bread should not be pre-sliced bread but whole-loaf so that the squares are thicker than a standard sliced bread.

Caprese Style Dipping Oil
by Deniese

INGREDIENTS

¼ cup Italian olive oil

A few drizzles red wine vinegar

2 tbls sun-dried tomatoes packed in oil, minced

1 tbls oil from the same jar

1 tbls dried basil or 2 tbls fresh

DIRECTIONS

1. Add all ingredients except vinegar into a wide, shallow serving dish. Mix lightly until tomatoes and herbs are incorporated. Let stand for an hour or more.

2. Just before serving drizzle red wine vinegar, letting it remain in little pockets.

This is great with an herbed focaccia bread, again cut into cubes and dipped.

Spicy Sherry Vinegar Dipping Oil
by Deniese

INGREDIENTS

½ cup extra virgin olive oil

A few drizzles sherry vinegar

1 lime, juice and some
    of the zest

2 large pinches red chili flakes

4 cloves garlic, minced

2 large pinches dried parsley or a
    small palmful of fresh

4 sprigs fresh parsley for garnish
    (optional)

DIRECTIONS

1. Juice the lime into a wide, shallow serving dish. Add minced garlic and let 'cook' for a few minutes. Add the rest of the ingredients except the sherry vinegar and parsley sprigs and mix so all are well absorbed and well distributed. Let stand for an hour or more.

2. Just before serving drizzle sherry vinegar, letting it remain in little pockets. Add parsley sprigs.

This dipping oil stands up great to a multigrain bread or dense rye.

CHAPTER 8
Death of a Legend

The raging bull I always saw my father as included his ruddy outdoor look even though he would have starved if he had ever been required to live off the land. He was not a hunter nor a fisherman nor a gardener and from what I could tell he did not even like the outdoor life unless he was gouging into it with a pick or shovel. He loved land, but only for what it could bring him — profit or security. But from my earliest memories, whenever we were outside he would thrust his face to the sun and bask in its tanning glory, eyes closed as if in rapture.

In 1982 my father announced that he was going into the hospital for a little surgery. He had a polyp in his sinuses that was causing him issues. Our local St. Helena Hospital was very good at the time and has gotten even better over the years so this was the logical choice. I don't remember anybody making a big deal out of what my father described as a routine procedure until the day after surgery. I don't remember how the news was delivered but the long and short of it was that after the surgery the doctor told my father to go home and get his things in order — he had only a couple months to live. The polyp had turned out to be a melanoma tumor that was inoperable. The surgeon had left the polyp in presumably because it would have been very difficult to remove and there was no point. Why spend the last few weeks of his life recovering from an extensive surgery when he needed to be saying his good-byes and straightening up his affairs?

Obviously we were all devastated by the news but my father was not about to go down without a fight. Probably pulling strings from his years of working in San Francisco, that next Monday Dad was at the University of San Francisco Medical Center. Within hours the word came back to the family that, indeed it was melanoma and indeed it was immediately life threatening but that the doctors there were certainly willing to see if they could remove it. Obviously my father agreed and the doctors pushed their schedules around to accommodate the four-hour surgery for the next day. I remember crowding into my father's hospital room after surgery, all family members who could possibly make it standing nervously around trying not to stare at this pale and diminished figure still mostly sleeping and completely helpless. My father was 62 and other than the normal flus and colds, to my knowledge he had enjoyed prefect health (oh, except that time I refused to sweep out one of the closets up at the Ranch and instead of me he had gotten

bitten by the black-widow spider that was living there).

The surgeon arrived after a long while and we woke Dad up for the prognosis. "We got the tumor," he announced. "I left you waiting for a while because we wanted to run the pathology before I came in to see you, but we got it all — clear margins all around. We don't even see where you will need chemo or radiation therapy." Dr. Crumbley became a comp guest of the Inn for life (he actually stopped coming after his fourth or fifth visit, probably because he was embarrassed that we never let him pay). We were all ecstatic with knee-buckling relief and, though my father was certainly not in any condition to party, the rest of us stayed while he dozed, soaking in the peppermint air of celebration (I don't know what that means but peppermint sounds like the right adjective here).

Sometime later in walked the surgeon from St. Helena Hospital, claiming that he had been in the area and thought he would stop by. How nice we all thought. But no, it appeared he had come to validate his original actions because the next thing that came out of his mouth was, "Well, I guess it's all well and good, but your father's quality of life is going to be pretty poor. With chemo and radiation therapies — well — he is going to spend his last days miserable." I think he had more to say, but he didn't get a chance. I am not a violent man but I have never come so close to picking up a person and pounding them through a wall. I don't remember touching this man and I don't remember exactly how he was ushered out of the room, but I do remember delivering a violent account of Dr. Crumbley's report that there would be no radiation or chemo therapy and that he had better leave.

My father recovered from the surgery quickly and though he had appeared to regain full health this seemed to be a turning point in his life. He officially retired and handed the reins of the family business to me and though he lived a hundred yards up the road from the Inn and I often found myself taking a stroll up the driveway to ask his advice, he actually did a pretty damn good job of retiring. You see, I think he had a little

information that he never shared with the rest of us, to my knowledge even my mother. To this day melanoma is not something you get over (I know because I ask my dermatologist three times a year when I go to visit him and every time he cuts another little growth off my body). Today there are drugs that can slow the progression of this disease, but there is no cure. It can metastasis years later in whatever organ it chooses. Apparently back then this disease was nothing but a wait and see game. This information either my father didn't know or he just failed to share it with the rest of us because eight years later it came as a complete surprise to me that the cancer had returned and that this time, indeed, it was inoperable. It had lodged primarily in his liver and was apparently a very painful disease at this point.

It was a very painful disease for all of us, but we had a little time. My father's primary concern (as it absolutely should have been) was to protect my mother and since I was running the family business and the rest of my siblings were not in the "business world" at that time I spent many hours over many weeks learning every intimate detail about my father's finances and the lengths to which he had gone to squirrel money and investments away from prying eyes, including my mother's. In fact, before he had divulged any of this to me he had demanded a sacred oath from me. Since neither of us were religious we had settle on an 'honor of a father to a son' oath. This promise was that I never let on to my mother the extent of the family finances (really to this day I have to tell you that they were not *that* extensive but my mother was only 66 at the time and I could see that great care would have to be taken to keep her financially secure) and that I keep her on a strict budget or she would blow through everything within a matter of a few years. Even on the very day I made this vow I knew this was patently absurd and I had no intention of keeping it, but I guess there are dysfunctions we each will take to our grave. It's not that there was absolutely enough money to keep my mother in whatever lifestyle she choose, but that my mother had never been a spendy kind of gal. Her only extravagances I was ever

aware of were a few politically motivated trips she had taken through the World Affairs Council of San Francisco to Russia and the Middle-East.

My father would prepare for these finance meetings by skipping his first two doses of morphine at breakfast and then at noon. By mid-afternoon he was in considerable pain but was clear-headed. We would spend an hour or so in the living room of the family home, him lying on the couch, me sitting in a chair taking notes, his voice hushed, his demeanor serious and secretive. We would go over the different real estate holdings he had (all small investments around the Napa Valley where he had brokered deals between someone with a great idea and someone with some money to invest and instead of taking a commission for his work he would take a small piece of the action and/or a management contract for the partnership that was created). We would talk about the people involved, the histories and the future potentials. He was thoroughly reluctant to hand any of this over to me. On a number of occasions he voiced his hesitancy, almost loathing to be asking me to take these responsibilities over. I felt I understood his feelings. I was going through a divorce at the time with my two children becoming more and more of a battleground and it was a lot to dump on me at the time. Finally, by the third or fourth time he voiced his reluctance I tried to ease his conscience, insisting that I could take this on and that it would not overwhelm me. A long, thoughtful, painful silence followed. I'm sure my father was terrified at what he needed to say next, but he didn't have time to teach me any more life lessons.

"Jim, if I could give these jobs to anyone else I would, but there is just no one else I trust to take care of these things. It is not that I don't think you can handle them or that I am asking too much of you, it is because the money is too easy. I'm afraid this work will spoil you."

"Wha-?" I remember stammering.

"Jim, some of these investments — all you have to do is collect the rent, balance the checkbook and send out checks to the investors every other month! And you skim 4 percent off the top. I'm afraid it's going to ruin you, make you lazy. I need

you hungry!" That was the end of that session. I had to suddenly take a walk.

A couple months later, under the wonderful care of Hospice Napa Valley, my father was told that he only had a day or so left. In a wonderful celebration of life the entire family gathered at the family home on Mother's Day weekend 1990. While pots and pans clattered and siblings and extended family caught up with each other, my father, absolutely convinced that he would not make it through the night, had a private audience with everyone in attendance. When it was my turn he was in my parent's bed, propped up with a number of pillows.

Not in a harsh way, but very directly my father asked, "What can I give you before I go?"

I balled up my courage and, remembering his comment of a few months earlier, said, "All I really want is for you to tell me I am doing all right in your eyes."

"I can't do that Jim," he stated flatly. "I don't agree with your choices." I'm sure he could see the hurt and confusion in my eyes. Maybe he was talking about the old me, the dissolute. But since those days I had gone back to college; I had gotten straight A's and graduated #1 in my class; I had returned to the Inn with a completely new work ethic, no longer judging my week by how many hours I put in but by how much I accomplished; I was becoming the man I knew he wanted me to be. Or, until that moment I thought I was. "I don't think you fully understand how difficult life can be and I don't think you are preparing for your future, so no, I can't give you any kind of blessing." My father paused again knowing I would need a moment or two to digest that harsh reality before I could hear what he had to say next. "The only thing I can say is that you can't look to me for acceptance. That's not where you should look. You have to find acceptance within yourself." I felt like that old Johnny Cash song where the dad had just named his kid 'Sue'. We talked a little more but I don't remember crying or complaining or raging though I felt like doing all three. And I don't know what he told his other kids. Maybe they didn't ask such a direct question or maybe they have told me over the years and my pain trumped anything they could

have said so I just don't remember, but these words reside deeply inside of me and for years after my father's death, when I was struggling with a problem at the Inn I would find myself literally half-way up the driveway to the family house before I would remember that he was no longer there to seek out his advice and approval. There's no doubt my father was a Depression baby and no matter how hard he tried to recreate the Depression for his children so he could pass on those most valuable lessons, he failed miserably. None of his children accept that happiness can only come from hard work and sacrifice, or that the almighty greenback is the only form of security. Each of his children has charted different paths and I honestly believe that if he were able to look down on us now, maybe freed from some of his earthly pain, he would see that all of his children have taken the better parts of what he was offering and forgiven him for trying to drive home what he considered to be his most urgent lessons.

More than 300 people showed up to my father's wake. It was held in a quiet

May drizzle in front of the family home. There is a wide gravel circular drive leading directly up to the front porch, with hundred-year-old gnarly oaks accenting the center of the circle and vineyards off to both sides. I don't remember that there were refreshments or food or anything other than folks showing up wanting to say goodbye. I think friends of my sister and brother showed up with instruments for some impromptu music.

I do remember my mother in tears and frustration coming up to me and saying, "If he only knew." When questioned further she elaborated, "Your father would be shocked at this. He had no idea so many people cared."

I have two stories about my father that have become lore in our family. The first one is ancient and possibly explains or at least softens the rather harsh feelings I had towards my father for many years after his death. From the stories I hear my father was about as good a student in school as I was, barely scraping by.

Researching this book I went back through all my old photo albums and found a stack of report cards from my grammar school days. "Jimmy is a pleasure to have in class and participates well in class discussions. Now if we could get him to actually complete his class work he could possibly become a fine student."

I don't have any of my father's old report cards but I do know that after high school he enrolled in the University of Wisconsin and within a year had flunked out. World War II was brewing, so instead of looking for a job he decided to enlist in the Army Air Force and take his chances there. Getting in early, he was a fully trained pilot by the time the shooting started and ended up spending the entire war in Texas as a flight instructor. When the war ended he was decommissioned in San Francisco and decided to take another shot at a higher education on the GI Bill and enrolled at UC Berkeley on the government's dime. The story goes that he was taking some business marketing class that asked the students to develop a product and then come up with a marketing plan to sell the product. My father was not proud of his work and when the instructor handed all the papers back except my father's he started getting quite nervous. Then the professor made eye contact with Dad, "Mr. Smith, I'd like to see you after class." Now my father knew it had not been a mistake and he started reliving the news he had gotten six years earlier when he had been dumped from the University of Wisconsin. But he was also a little confused. He knew his marketing plan had been weak but he actually thought his product had been pretty slick. He hung back and waited for everyone to vacate the room before he approached his professor who had not looked up, apparently giving Dad's paper one more go-over.

"Mr. Smith, where did you come up with this idea?" he asked, finally making eye contact.

"Well," my father fidgeted. "I go to the Cal football games and everybody is wearing those little rooter's caps, you know the little beanies with the short little bills."

"I know what a rooter's cap is Mr. Smith," he replied impatiently.

My father continued nervously, "I noticed that as the sun gets low everybody sticks their programs up under their hats to shade their eyes. I thought if I just extended the bill of the cap a few inches the hats could have built-in shade."

"Your marketing plan is weak," the professor commented. "I gave you a C on that part of the assignment, but I don't care what you do, skip class, drop out of school, whatever it takes, you have to find somebody to bankroll this idea and get it out as soon as you can. You have pure gold here. Do not tell ANYBODY about this idea and go find some money."

My father was thrilled and immediately called his somewhat estranged father, who was the only person he knew who had any money. As Dad told the story, his father wouldn't even discuss the idea with him so a couple years later someone else came out with the modern day baseball cap.

———————

The other story has a happier ending. As I have mentioned previously we had a 120-acre ranch in the coastal mountains of Sonoma County above a major tributary to the Russian River called Dry Creek (I guess it was pretty dry in the summer). Anyway, I guess the Federal or State government along with the Army Corp of Engineers had decided to dam up the river and create a lake. My father was not pleased. Our property was going to be close to the lake but not on it so all my father could think about was getting all the noise from all the motor boats and none of the benefit of having water-front property. He did some research and learned that the lake was going to have two distinct arms. He mulled this over for a few weeks, did some more research and jumped in his car for a drive to San Francisco where the Army Corps of Engineers had its primary offices. He went through the registry of employees and found the office listing of the guy he was looking for. Balling up all his charismatic energy he stormed the floor, blowing past the secretary, down the hall and into the head engineer's office, his hand extended in glee and adulation. "I just had to come and congratulate you in person." the man couldn't stand fast enough for my father to be on him, all smiles and enthusiasm. The man was a civil servant, what else was he going to do but accept the praise and return a hearty handshake. Before the man could even start to ask what he had done to deserve this praise my father told him. "I have been told that you were the man responsible for the brilliant idea for Lake Sonoma. I am an avid fisherman and your idea is going to make history. To segregate it into two distinct uses with motorized boats on the north branch and the south branch being dedicated to peace and tranquility AND PROPER FISHING, it's brilliant!"

The man nodded and accepted the adulation, offering my father a chair to discuss what further refinement this avid fisherman might be able to add to his idea. To my knowledge, fifty years later the lake is still segregated in this way.

Clam Dip

by Gramma Nummy

Gramma Nummy

This recipe goes back too far for me to remember who first brought it to the table but I'm pretty sure we need to credit at least the original recipe to my grandmother Nummy. I remember Nummy as a bitter and humorless woman except when she and I were playing Canasta, a card game that I would love to reinstitute somehow back into my family. I think I was the only one of the kids who would play this game with her so I think I stole a huge chunk of the little charity this woman possessed. But if she brought this clam dip into the Smith family repertoire she needs some added creds.

INGREDIENTS

8 ozs cream cheese

8 ozs mayonnaise

1 small can chopped claims, drained except for a tiny bit

1 tsp Worcestershire sauce

1 clove garlic

1 tsp lemon juice

½ tsp salt

DIRECTIONS

1. Remove cream cheese from the refrigerator a few hours before preparation.

2. Chop or crush garlic and combine with lemon juice while you are getting the other ingredients organized, giving the garlic just a little resident time with the lemon juice to chemically "cook" the garlic a little.

3. Place the cream cheese on a large plate and work it with a fork until it is velvety smooth. Slowly add the mayonnaise to the cream cheese, working it constantly into a smooth loose

mixture. Add just a hint of the clam juice and the Worcestershire sauce as you go, incorporating it completely. Add the fully drained clams and incorporate them.

4. Refrigerate for an hour or so before serving, but not too long. Fully refrigerated clam dip will be hard to dip into and will really not maximize the flavors.

So, that's the original recipe, but if you have had this dip at the Inn and liked it, this one will leave you flat. Quadruple the garlic and add some smoky or spicy paprika and you will be closer to what we serve at the Inn. I usually make at least a double batch when I'm making it at home and if I have family coming over I stick closer to the original recipe, but if I have friends coming over that are not stifled by the family traditions I'll play around and add smoked clams or smoked oysters, fresh uncooked corn straight off the cob or a ¼ cup of chopped roasted red bell peppers. I think I'll try minced chives next time.

My father and I had completely different tastes in food. Where I could almost completely live on Mexican food, my father could not tolerate anything quite so ethnic. In fact he even shied away from Italian and thought French was just too fancy (read expensive). He was a Mid-Western meat and potatoes kind of guy. Once we started serving a full breakfast at the Inn I developed the following recipe specifically for him. Noticed no garlic. I think this is one of the only dishes I have created that doesn't have at least a touch of garlic, but my father really did not cotton to garlic in his food.

Sausage & Eggs Casserole

by Jim

INGREDIENTS

12 eggs

1 lb pork sausage (recipe
        to follow)

1 ½ cups milk

4 cups cheddar cheese

1 tsp dry mustard

15 slices sourdough bread

½ onion, chopped

½ lb mushrooms, sliced

DIRECTIONS

1. Preheat oven to 325 degrees.

2. Sauté sausage until lightly browned. Add mushrooms and
    onions and sauté until browned. Drain whatever fat is left.

3. In a large bowl beat eggs, then add milk and mustard and
    incorporate. Add sausage mixture, cheese and bread to
    the bowl, making sure bread is well disbursed and coated
    with liquid. Pour into greased large baking dish.

4. Bake approximately 40 — 45 minutes until eggs are firm
    and set. Let cool 10 minutes and serve in 3 inch squares.

My father insisted on a large dollop of sour cream on top.

Italian Sausage
by Jim

INGREDIENTS

3 lbs pork shoulder (as discussed in a previous recipe, ground pork makes the process a lot easier but then you are losing some of that control, but for the first few times you might want to just use ground pork)

¼ cup olive oil (omitted if using ground pork)

10 cloves garlic, minced (omitted when making it for my father)

2 tsps grey salt

1 tsp cayenne pepper, ground

1 tbls fennel seed, whole

2 tbls red pepper flakes

1 tsp black pepper

½ cup red wine

DIRECTIONS

1. Cut pork into 1 inch cubes, removing as much fat as you feel is appropriate. Add meat and olive oil to a food processor and pulse the blades until meat is ground.

2. We like to toast all the spices before adding them to the meat. In the skillet, place all spices over medium heat and toast until aromatic.

3. Add all ingredients to the food processor and pulse until well mixed. Set aside at least overnight before adding to your favorite recipe.

CHAPTER 9

Napa Valley —
Fertile Fields for Innovation

The food and wine scene in the Napa Valley is an ever-changing wildly innovative landscape. Subtlety and tradition are attributes that are mostly seen as connoting a lack of flavor or imagination. New, exciting, different — these are the adjectives Napans favor and I feel this is one of the reasons so many folks flock here to visit or to live. And though the Inn does not have a cutting edge restaurant that doesn't mean we don't take the food that we serve seriously. Like, for instance, last year we planted over 300 tomato plants of a dozen or so current and heirloom varieties, 300 pepper plants from sweet and mild to screaming hot, as well as a large field

of fun varieties of cucumbers, zucchini, various melons and a fascinating variety of pumpkins and gourds for our fall decorations. Many guests are amazed that our small Inn, which is still run on the B&B style of supplying a great, free breakfast and wine & appetizers in the afternoon, but no actual restaurant that we can go through so much produce. But we do, we don't waste any of that precious vine-ripened deliciousness. That doesn't mean that two or three times every summer we aren't completely overwhelmed with produce but it does mean that sometimes we need to get a little creative with what we do with, say, 200 pounds of tomatoes and peppers that just came in from the gardens.

But before I start telling you about all the wonderful things we make with this produce I have a confession to make. I was born with a deficient tongue, something I have been ashamed about since at least my early twenties, you know, when you really start needing a talented tongue. But when I finally — I mean well into my forties — learned the truth I was greatly relieved and since have fully come out of the closet. I am going to pass this little secret along now, because — well — I think I might be able to help others.

I was apparently quite shorted when it comes to taste buds. There, I said it. In the Napa Valley wine and food scene this has been an immense challenge and has caused more than a little shame from time to time. You know, when the guy sitting next to you is expounding, "Are you picking up the hints of deeply ripened honeydew?" or "I'm getting floral notes of honeysuckle with maybe a little jasmine."

"Yeah, smells good," is all I can counter if I'm being honest, because that is all I can smell. "Smells *really* good! Is this a Cabernet or a Zinfandel?" is what I really want to say.

Wikipedia reports that humans have an average of from 3,000 to 10,000 taste receptors in our mouths. Though whoever wrote this entry obviously doesn't know what an "average" is (I may not be able to distinguish honeysuckle from rose, but I can do math) the article certainly points out that there is a huge spread between people. Some people have three times the number of taste buds as others and I am absolutely positive I am on the low end of that spectrum. One of the characteristics of someone with low-t(astebuds) is that they love big flavors, spicy food and tequila (at least that's my excuse). Folks with a plethora of taste buds tend more towards subtle, layered flavors and many are overwhelmed by the big spicy dishes. Apparently there are also large differences in olfactory capabilities, so that adds even more to the variations.

That's not to say that I don't love Napa Valley wines and great food but what it does say is that I'm never going to be that guy who says (unless I am completely B.S.ing) "Oh, are you getting the undertones of cassis and black fruit?" I might be able to get to, "Boy, that's a mouthful," or

"This wine lays a little flat on my tongue, not much of a finish."

Our Chef Ryan doesn't seem to fit this profile as clearly as I do. Though he can talk the talk and walk the walk with the best of them he is still into big flavors, so I still think he might be a little low on "T", but who am I to judge. He likes big flavors so we get along just fine.

From early July sometimes through as late as Halloween we are harvesting, serving, juicing, cooking and freezing bins upon bins full of fresh-off-the-vine produce that we have grown. Everything we can find an immediate use for we serve as unprocessed as possible: sliced tomatoes that are so red they are almost purple that have never, ever seen a refrigerator, julienned colored sweet peppers so shiny and bright they look like they have been waxed, partially peeled cucumbers just slightly chilled and drizzled with a little extra virgin and balsamic, honeydew and cantaloupe simply quartered and garnished with mint from right outside the backdoor. But that can't keep up with the piles the gardens are producing so I jump in. Through the summer and into the fall I make two or three batches of my homemade salsa. It is amazing how many things you can put salsa on if it is knock-your-socks-off fresh salsa. Chef makes his own versions of salsas as well so it is not uncommon to have a good-natured guest taste-off every few nights.

Then there is our Bloody-Mary mix. For a few weeks, usually from early August into late September, we have enough produce to make the ugliest, best tasting Bloody-Marys I can imagine. I say 'ugly' because the mix is not bright red, thick and fully homogenized like you find in stores. It has so many colors of produce in it and the produce is so juicy that it turns out more brownish/red and a little watery, with a tendency to separate if it sits for more than a few minutes. But with a healthy shot of locally-made Charbay vodka and a couple shakes of one of Chef's homemade hot sauces, well, it gets another day of vacation off to a mighty fine start.

Even with all this usage we are often still drowning. That's when we get the barbeque and the smoker fired up. I gotta say, before this new-found wealth I would never have thought of completely filling a large BBQ and an even larger smoker with tomatoes, peppers, onions and garlic, but it is amazing what can come of such insanity. Chef will usually just give this stuff a quick smoke and a bit of roasting before he brings it in for the tomato sauce he will cook up in huge batches to use and/or freeze so that guests who

come other times of the year can still enjoy this bounty. But if I have my way with some of this over-flow I will likely leave everything on at about 170 degrees for the whole night. This is in preparation to make my almost famous STP (smoky tomato paste) which we also use all year long. All these dehydrated veggies (they come off the barbeque like sun-dried tomatoes) whirled together with a little salt and molasses and OMG you have just created a spicy thick condiment that can be added to almost any sauce for a little extra kick or just spread on a burger bun instead of some runny catsup. This would be an extravagance beyond almost any budget except when you grow your own.

Like any innkeeper there is an undefined overlap between my business life and my home life. Many of the culinary experiments Chef or I make at the Inn make their way to my home and visa-versa. Fortunately my wife and family are also into the big flavors I love so our home larder, refrigerator and wine cellar reflect that, filling each to overflowing with fun little treasures. I can't tell you how much endless crap we get from friends who look into our refrigerator. My wife and I throw a lot of parties and one common theme is that there is never enough room in our refrigerator for the stuff our guests bring with them. For instance most of our friends know we don't drink much beer and so will show up with a 6-pack or two. Nope, no room. Let's get out the ice chest because their damn refrigerator is jammed with who knows what!

Well, I'll tell you what. I'll walk in there right now and tell you. The whole door of the fridge is crammed to bursting with condiments. Right now I have seven different mustards, none of which are French's. I've got two dijons, a honey, something from Gilroy (the garlic capital of the world), one with soy and ginger, Coleman's, and another one I think I'll throw out. I have one whole shelf of salad dressings I know nothing about (my wife does the salads and they are always so good I just don't ask) and another shelf for our drink concentrates and bubbly water. We have our own bubbly water maker and my daughter and I have two go-to recipes (my wife is fine with regular water). One is our lemon-aide which is a

couple tablespoons of lemon concentrate (if our Meyer lemon tree is out) two big pumps of Torani's French Vanilla syrup and fill the rest of a large glass with ice and bubbly water. Our other house drink is about 1/3 to 2/3s Pom to bubbly water (no sodas allowed in this house except maybe every once in a while one or two of those delicious artisan root beers that are flooding the shelves). The last shelf is standard stuff like catsup, different oils we refrigerate, soy sauce, stuff like that.

But the main shelves are crammed, too, and this is where the real fun lives. Butter, I have six versions of butter at the moment. Regular everyday butter, some Irish butter we like a lot (I guess my retarded tongue just doesn't get unsalted butter so these are both salted), a small Pyrex dish of clarified butter and two different types of homemade garlic butter, one where the garlic and butter were separated after roasting the garlic and one where the two were whirled together after roast-ing. At the moment I also have a small tub of spicy bacon-butter. This was left-over from the bacon popcorn I made for the Inn's Christmas party (I have not yet decided if I am going to give out this recipe, but think about bacon, popcorn and spices and let your imagination take you away). I am writing this chapter on January 3, 2015 so I hate to think what my cholesterol levels are right now, after the holidays, but mostly we use all of these condiments sparingly, but they are always at the ready. Then, of course, the garlic that I roasted and separated has been whirled into its own paste.

I always have two different types of caramelized onions at hand, one with the onions still in long strands and one where I have whirled them into a paste. I have four or five different kinds of olives, but other than the Costco-sized jar of martini olives these kind of come a go. Lately my daughter and I have been on the "best hot dog" search. It seems that all of a sudden (or maybe I just wasn't paying attention since hot dogs have never been high on my list) all sorts of new artisan hot dogs appeared. Lately it is one of the only proteins I can get my 13-year-old daughter to eat — plus it is just way fun to have something culinary to explore with her — so I have also started making my own relishes to go with the four brands of hot dogs currently in the meat compartment (including a Kobe-beef dog that really wasn't very good). A crisp dill relish in the refrigerator section of the store is all well and fine, but once I throw in some fresh onion, roasted red bell pepper or jarred jalapeno or pepperoncini, it rocks! And then with a little Coleman's mustard my relish takes on a whole new face. Then I made up a relish that doesn't have pickles at all. It has finely chopped sun-dried tomatoes, roasted sweet bell peppers of varying colors, a touch of my smoky tomato paste (house-made last summer when my gardens were overflowing with tomatoes and peppers), a little of the chopped caramelized onions, some dried lemon peel that lives in my spice rack and a little of the roasted garlic. Then, for a little more punch, I threw in some Hungarian paprika and a few shakes of true balsamic vinegar and a fair bit of Apple Farm Apple Cider Vinegar. Wow, straight on a toasted dog bun or add a little mayo for a burger bun!

The only other interesting thing that really needs to live in my refrigerator is

Buster's BBQ Sauce. Up in Calistoga, about seven miles from the Inn is this funky little drive-in called Buster's Southern BBQ. Buster is a former 49er lineman who makes the best BBQ I have ever had. Now, granted this is not huge BBQ territory, Texas, the South, the Midwest may have it all over us when it comes to BBQ, but at least for me this is the best. He does chicken and ribs and pork loin which are all good, but in my opinion the Tri-tip is the way to go. He has an outdoor standing BBQ grill that is probably 5'X5' square with the grill at least 2' from the coals and it is always packed with 30 or 40 roasting Tri-tip roasts. I have recently learned that the beef Tri-tip cut is not as common outside of California but this is a wonderful cut that is kind of a cross between a steak and a roast. It is a triangular shaped cut from the bottom sirloin that at least Wikipedia says most parts of the country either grind into hamburger or cut into smaller steaks. I buy these babies three or four two-packs at a time at Costco and stick into my freezer to pull about one a week out for one dinner and three or four lunches. Chef Ryan also serves Tri-tip as

one of the choices for the Inn's day-tour service (Inn-Cursions).

But back to Busters! I'm sure the slow cooking of the Tri-tip has something to do with its tremendous success, but for me it's the sauce. He has two intensities, mild and burn your face off hot. The Tri-tip is served very simply on a toasted soft French roll, open-faced with the sauce ladled over the top (I get a side of his coleslaw to help put some of the fire out). I get them to give me half hot and half mild though they usually cheat a little towards more mild and that works out fine. Most eat it open-faced with a knife and fork. Though I seldom make a special trip to enjoy this treat, any time I am planning a trip that takes me by Buster's I will try to time my passing to be around lunchtime. But he might have lost himself some business because recently he started selling the BBQ sauce in jars (they are canning jars but they are not heat sealed. I think they should be heat sealed but I haven't gotten sick yet!) so when I go for lunch I also pick up one hot and two mild jars that I can take home, mix and refrigerate for my own Tri-tip lunches. If you go on-line you can get their number. They will mail you the sauce.

Word to the wise, if you plan to visit Buster's on your next trip to Napa Valley pretty much every Saturday and Sunday is absolutely packed with motorcycle clubs from all over the state that have this spot as their turn-around destination.

Pan Roasted Garlic

INGREDIENTS

2 lbs peeled Costco garlic

2 lbs butter

DIRECTIONS

1. Dump the garlic into a standard cast iron pan, turn on the heat and throw a pound or two of butter in.

2. Once the butter melts lower heat and cook on stove top (stirring occasionally) until cloves are golden brown and soft. I say a pound or two because it is all up to you what you want to use it for.

Personally, when I get a bag of garlic at Costco (3 lbs) it is going to go bad before I can use even half of it so I take about 20 cloves out for general use and then roast the rest of the bag in two batches. One batch I use half the bag of garlic and one pound of butter. This one I will whirl together and stir while it cools so the mixture stay somewhat mixed (in the morning it has usually separated a bit). The other batch I will cook in more butter and once roasted will separate out the garlic (note: most of the milk solids from the butter tends to go with the garlic so you pretty much end up with clarified garlic butter). Sometimes I will whirl the garlic into a paste and sometimes not, depending on how much I want to clean the blender yet again!

Caramelized Onions

by Jim

INGREDIENTS

6 to 8 large yellow onions

1/3 cup vegetable oil

1/3 cup Balsamic vinegar

Salt to taste

Fresh cracked black
pepper to taste

DIRECTIONS

1. Chop onions across the grain into long straight strips.

2. Since I have never mastered stir-fry this is pretty much the only thing I still use my wok for. Place oil in wok (or any large non-reactive pan) and heat. Add onions, salt and pepper liberally and mix with oil.

3. Reduce heat and cook slowly until onions have released almost all of their moisture and are a deep brown in color (about 1 ½ hours).

4. Add Balsamic if desired and cook away the liquid while coating the onions in the reduced vinegar.

5. I then take half of the cooked onions and whirl them into a paste while the other half I leave in strands for dishes like my Kick-Ass Sea Bass you read about earlier in this book.

Roasted Garlic and Caramelized Onion Dip

By Ryan

A favorite with our guests and any party my wife and I throw.

INGREDIENTS

¼ cup roasted garlic paste
  (recipe above)

¼ cup caramelized onion paste
  (recipe above)

1 ½ cups sour cream

8 oz cream cheese

1 tbls fresh parsley

½ tsp Worcestershire sauce

DIRECTIONS

1. Remove cream cheese from refrigerator a few hours before preparation. Place cream cheese on a plate and work with a fork until it is smooth and creamy.

2. Slowly add garlic paste and then onion paste, working into the cream cheese until smooth and a little loose.

3. Season with the Worcestershire sauce, then mix in the sour cream. Garnish with coarsely chopped parsley.

Roasted Garlic and Caramelized Onion Scrambled Eggs

By Jim

A couple of Sundays ago I was scrounging around in the refrigerator looking for something different to cook for breakfast. My wife makes great breakfast goulashes by frying up all sorts of leftovers that I would never put together, throwing in a couple eggs and calling it good. And it *is* almost always *good*. I knew we had an ear of corn and a half an onion as well as some brown eggs I had gotten a day after they were laid. Then it hit me, why use the rather plain onion when I have a Tupperware full of my caramelized onions? And wait, I have a tub of roasted garlic too!

INGREDIENTS

4 eggs

4 strips of bacon

1 cob of corn, kernels cut off the cob

1 tsp caramelized onion paste

1 tsp roasted garlic paste

2 dollops whatever salsa you might have

2 tbls goat cheese

DIRECTIONS

1. Fry bacon crispy and crumble.

2. Add the two pastes to a bowl. Crack one egg into bowl and mix to loosen up the pastes. Add another eggs and keep loosening the pastes (so they don't clump). Add the other two eggs and mix well.

3. Add bacon (personally I would be using the bacon grease to be frying up some red potatoes, but that's maybe just me) and mix.

4. Throw a little of the bacon grease in a pan over high heat and add corn. Brown the corn slightly before adding the egg mixture.

5. Lower the heat and scramble eggs to desired doneness. Plate and garnish with salsa and goat cheese.

We actually used sour cream as a garnish the first time, but discovered that goat cheese was much better the next time we made this. Who knows what we will discover next?

Beef Rub
by Brother Jeff

INGREDIENTS

½ cup mild chili powder

½ cup cumin

½ cup smoky paprika

½ cup garlic salt

DIRECTIONS

1. Mix all ingredients together and store sealed in a cool dry place.

Rubbed Beef Tri-tip

Choose a 2 ½ lb Beef Tri-tip (I always choose the biggest ones I can find so they can roast a little longer. If purchased from a regular butcher this cut may have a large fat cap that you can either choose to cut off before or after cooking depending on how fatty you want your served meat to be. It cooks up just fine without 90% of that fat layer).

Pull Tri-tip from the refrigerator a couple hours before roasting if possible. Rub generously all the way around with the rub mentioned above. Let stand for another hour out of refrigeration if possible. If I am feeling frisky, or having friends over and really want to do this right I will get my Big Green Egg fired up by letting regular, though very short cut, split oak logs burn down to coals. With vents open place the meat on the grill for about 15 minutes on the first side (or until deeply browned) turn it over and close the vents almost completely to finish it to about 125 degrees internally (maybe about 10 minutes, but it all depends on how hot the fire was when you started). Let it sit for a good 20 minutes before carving across the grain. If I am not feeling so ambitious I will use the same process in the oven with the meat on a broiler pan on the middle rack, with the oven set to 450 degrees on broil. Heat a little of the Buster's BBQ sauce to pour over the meat once it is sliced and plated.

CHAPTER 10

The Deflowering of The Inn

First my mom was the decorator (along with her good friend Sally) for the Inn, then it was my sister and now it is my daughter, all very accomplished artists and all with at least some formal training in decorating. And then there's me, the guy who needs to be somewhat practical when it comes to running a hotel and really values comfort over design. The decorating "battles" have been — and hopefully always will be — endless and have mostly all ended in negotiated truces (read they got their way at least 80 percent of the time).

When we first opened the Inn wallpaper was all the rage for inns such as ours. Every room had at least an accent of wallpaper with many of the rooms having all the walls papered. I remember visiting another inn in the Valley where the innkeepers boasted that they had three different wallpapers in every room, the main room, the bathroom and the closet. Though we didn't go to that extreme, wallpaper was prevalent throughout the Inn.

The following three photos should give you a little perspective on how the room décor and amenities have changed over the years. Though we still get the occasional ding on TripAdvisor or Yelp or one of those other review sites I think you will see that our rooms are regularly updated and upgraded, just not in a modern fashion. We still feel strongly that there is a substantial segment of the market that appreciates the non-cookie-cutter style of our rooms and will search us out for just that. BUT, we do have to keep up with the times a little bit. Property-wide, fast Wifi, raised plugs for easy device recharging (though in ten years people will say 'look, how quaint'), improved air conditioning, improved soundproofing, upgraded windows and doors, updated and improved window dressings (black-out curtains for those mornings after all that wine tasting), bathroom remodels, etc., etc.

The first photo is just a snapshot of Room 9, taken to document the furnishings

for insurance purposes, but it was the only one I had to show the transformation over the years of one particular room. Note the wallpaper, Gramma Nummy's stitcheries, a print my mother sliced out of some art book, wicker chair, table skirt, woven wood shades and a retrofitted air conditioner to somewhat cool the room. Since the air conditioner was there I guess that this shot was taken in the mid-80's when the rate for this room was probably around $87 (I never used round numbers because odd numbers looked more scientific, like I was setting the rates down to the gnat's ass).

If you can ignore the couple having an impromptu picnic in the next photo you will note that the wallpaper is gone, replaced by a wonderful plaster texture that set us back a fair penny, but the wicker and stitcheries are still there. Plaster, I love it! And though it is way more expensive to apply than regular drywall texture (mud) it has a depth of color and a true vintage feel that cannot be duplicated with other products. This photo was taken around 2004 when this room went for about $230.

rooms was replaced by comfy upholstered chairs and loveseats until just a few years ago — after my mother had officially retired at the age of 85 — I made an all-out attack on the remaining wicker. I think, on our 40th anniversary, there are only two or three pieces left but those are sturdy, good-looking chairs that can handle my ever-expanding size.

Additionally, I don't think I have acknowledged this, but I have never liked wicker furniture all that much, and there was a lot of it in our rooms when I first took over the Inn. I say "took over" meaning I started doing the lion's share of the work but my parents still held tightly to the reins. There was no doubt in anyone's minds that my mother was still the decorator. But I'm sorry, a 6'2" 200-pound man is just not comfortable sitting in a dainty wicker chair or a squeaking rattan couch. That's like telling me to drink a nice cup of tea with my pinkie out, it's just not going to happen. Fortunately, wicker breaks and it can only be repaired so many times. Slowly, ever so slowly, the wicker in the

In the next picture note the new door and windows, new drapes, new (old) desk, no wicker and no flowery quilt. A whole different feel to the room but still family artwork on the walls, the same bed (no, not the same mattress) and a similar country feel.

One battle we have not had to wage is over the wall-hangings. Heritage still reigns supreme here. Originally the walls of the guest rooms and common areas were adorned with every medium of family-made artwork: oils, watercolors, acrylics, photography and most famously

needlework. Contributions were made by my mother (if you see an unsigned piece around the Inn it's hers), my sister, my grandmother, my wife at the time, my mother-in-law, my sister-in-law, my brother and more recently my daughter and myself. Great pride has been taken with these pieces and most have survived the test of time, at least for us! Of course now, with more and more of our reservations coming through anonymous sources like Expedia and Hotels.com we are having to rethink the hominess of our rooms. It used to be that our guests were fully fore-warned that these were not your typical hotel rooms so they came prepared (or sought us out) with that in mind. Today that is just not the case. Word of mouth seems to be dying (the closest thing these days

is Facebook) and more and more of our guests are downright shocked that every room doesn't have a king-sized bed, a modern-looking slick bathroom and most shocking, a TV! We have gotten away with this heresy for forty years now, but I feel those days are numbered. One 2-Star rating on TripAdvisor or Expedia sets our marketing plan back a big chunk and if folks don't know they are booking a hotel without a TV (even though we do our best to inform them of this) I fully understand why some people are disappointed or just don't get why we don't have them.

So why don't we have TVs? Generally speaking, we rent rooms to women. Women are much more inclined to have romantic notions and their romantic notions for the most part do not include curling up with a warm remote or a husband that is carrying on their nightly tradition of falling asleep to the news. I can't tell you how many women over the years have come to check-out with an appreciative grin on their face and a confidential hand on my arm. "Thank you so much for not having TVs in your rooms." And since I am all about pleasing women this is all I need to hear.

If you have made it this far through this book I feel you might have a vested interest in these issues. You have either stayed with us or you are interested in the subject of innkeeping and what it takes to run a successful inn. TV, king-sized beds, broadband, a newspaper at your door in the morning, these all appear to me musts these days if you are trying to include the word "luxury" in any of your marketing, but are they? I'd really like to hear. I want to create an environment that is comfortable and nurturing to your romantic sides but that is definitely a moving target, both over the years and from couple to couple. So, how about you put the book down and pick up one of your devices, hop on Facebook and start a dialog. If you scroll down a bit maybe there is already one going, but wouldn't it be fun to be involved in the next version of the Inn?

Bell service is an amenity that has really surprised me over the years. I certainly appreciate bell service when I travel and yet my wife hates it. She really doesn't want anybody else touching her stuff and almost seems to find it demeaning to have strangers help her in that way. I say bring it on! But we have tried to institute bell service at the Inn at least five times over the years and the vast majority of guests decline if asked and seem put out if we just have it part of the system. Feel free to weigh in on that one too.

So, what are the amenities *I* think are important to include in a stay at The Wine Country Inn? The first — and last — and everything in between revolves around connection, genuine honest connection. And whether that connection comes in human form by a genuinely friendly smile at check-in, a comforting taste of food and wine at our wine social, the fact that we care enough to drive you to dinner and back so you'll get home safely (and you don't have to flip a coin to see who only gets one glass of wine), a greeting from the chef in the morning as the smells of wonderfully prepared food waft over you or the amazing connection you can feel to 'place' as you look out over vineyards and mountains instead of asphalt or city streets. Of course then there is the connection we are hoping you find with your partner: snuggling in front of a crackling fire instead of the all-consuming TV, sitting out on a balcony surrounded by vineyards or finding the secluded swing down almost in the vines or the deserted hot tub late in the evening with a blanket of stars overhead. Vacations are wonderful opportunities to reconnect and I have made it my life's mission to facilitate that as much as I can.

But I *do* feel the human connection is foremost. I know that is not what most people are actively looking for when they are choosing a hotel and what stands out for most on a website is: the thousand-count sheets, luxury-brand toiletries, dazzling artwork on the walls and from that you can assume aloofly elegant service. I'm sorry, but for me, those things are nice (except the aloof service) but they just leave me cold. Do I have to dress elegantly for breakfast? On vacation? I have had more than one of my silent partners insist that it is ludicrous to think that guests are checking into the Inn looking to strike up a friendship with the desk clerk or the chef or the innkeeper. I just shrug my shoulders and say, "I have seen it too many times to deny what I see. Maybe that's why Cheers! ran for as many seasons as it did. 'Where everybody knows your name, and they're always glad you came.'

History is another huge connection; an amenity that is hard to put into words. The Wine Country Inn has had four generations of Smiths involved, it has been owned by the same family for 40 years: husbands and wives, parents and children, sisters and brothers, cousins and nephews have all worked together to make this such a special place. And there is a certain part of our society that craves this, maybe a little part of each one of us. When I travel, even only as far as Napa I can feel the shift. New shopping developments with a lovely Whole Foods with a Trader Joe's a couple of stores down. Across the town is an In-And-Out (which I have to say I do crave every once in a while), something called Ulta that my wife loves and maybe people develop their own *connection* to these places, but none of them have history, none of them have family, at least not that you can touch. Even the architecture, the building materials scream of corporate efficiency, of squeezing the last buck out of the pickle jar. I can just see the MBAs in their spacious clean offices overlooking most any city, with their computer models and their sharpened pencils (I guess we have to come up with a new analogy for this concept) developing a staffing model that minimizes the human expense while uncaringly increasing the human cost.

I recently had one of my partners tell me he thinks many people probably stay at the Inn in spite of the décor and amenities in the rooms not because of them. After some thought I had to agree that that was probably true for a certain segment of our guests, but that the real question then is why would they come back at all? I went on to postulate that *authenticity* may well be the key to the comfort these folks feel. It is certainly what I feel at the Inn and I am betting ("albeit with your money too," I said to my partner) that the uniqueness and basic vision I have for the Inn will trump our shortcomings and we will come out just fine while at the same time giving something very special back to those who crave just a little more connection in their lives.

So, maybe we didn't "deflower the Inn" as the name of this chapter implies. We took the flowery wallpaper and patch-work quilts out, but hopefully not her innocence.

This chapter is screaming for a little comfort food so here are a few recipes.

Quick Chicken Noodle Soup

by Jim

Have I mentioned that I can rarely get my 13-year-old daughter to eat anything in the morning before toddling off to school? If she does, and I were to give her a choice, she's would eat some sugary muffin or pop-tart that's going to last her maybe an hour. On a whim, over a year ago, I bought some canned chicken at Costco and it sat up in my cupboard untouched. I guess I was thinking I would use it instead of tuna at some point when I was craving a comfortable tuna sandwich. But it turns out, on those three or four times a year that I am in the mood for a tuna sandwich I want a tuna sandwich. So this canned chicken just sat there. One morning I was desperate to get some food into my daughter before school (my wife heads off to work at 6 so it's on me). Anyway, I grabbed this can of chicken, threw some olive oil in a small kettle and started browning it. I still wasn't sure what I was doing, but after I browned it, somewhat reluctantly, I tasted it. It was tender and moist, well browned and a little salty. In other words it was pretty dang good. "My daughter loves soup" sprang into my head. I threw in a couple cups of water, pulled out some chicken base they also sell at Costco, then my Tupperware container of roasted garlic and voila!! Soup. I then found half a box of dry noodles that weren't really enough to make a full meal from and threw those in once my concoction was boiling. It was such a hit that now sometimes I get up at 5ish to make a batch for the whole family before we take off for work.

INGREDIENTS

1 can chicken chunks from
   Costco, drained

2 tbls chicken base from Costco

2 tbls olive oil or garlic butter

2 tbls roasted garlic paste from
   your refrigerator

4 cups water

Macaroni, any kind you have
   laying around

DIRECTIONS

1. Heat olive oil or butter in a sauce pan.

2. Add chicken and brown thoroughly (or for as long as you
    have time for). Add water and start heating. Add chicken
    broth and roasted garlic paste.

3. As it cooks taste for other spices you might want to add,
    a little curry powder if you're in the mood, a little cayenne
    or my new favorite Hungarian paprika.

4. Once it comes to a boil add pasta and cook until al dente.
    Done, serve it, eat it and go to work.

Who says breakfast has to be "breakfast food"?

Tater Babies

by Deniese

INGREDIENTS

5 lbs red potatoes, all
  walnut sized

1 ½ cups jack cheese, shredded

1 ½ cups cheddar
  cheese, shredded

1 ½ cups fried and
  crumbled bacon

3 tbls butter, melted

¼ cup dark mustard

½ cup chives, chopped

2 tbls garlic olive oil

1 tsp Worcestershire sauce

Sour cream to garnish

Chili Crunch in front with my collection of salts and my favorite bread in the background.

DIRECTIONS

1. Pre-heat oven to 350 degrees.

2. Prepare potatoes by cutting them in half and hollowing out the centers, leaving about ¼ inch of the flesh.

3. In a bowl mix the butter, oil and mustard. Place all the potato skins in the bowl and toss in the mustard mixture, making sure they are all well coated.

4. Place potatoes cut side down on a baking sheet and bake 15 – 20 minutes until the edges are crisp. Remove from oven and let cool.

5. In a food processor pulse cheese, then toss in bacon bits, Worcestershire sauce and chives.

6. Stuff skins with generous amounts of filling and place back onto cookie sheet, stuffed side up. Bake for 5 minutes until cheese is well melted. Serve hot with a dollop of sour cream.

Personally I like a little bit more of a kick to this recipe. During my last visit to Dean & Deluca I found this amazing condiment called Chile Crunch made by Chile Colonial out of Denver. http://www.chilecrunch.com/. I mixed a little of this into the sour cream and served this recipe at my mother's 90th birthday. My brother took one bite and said, "I see you discovered 'Chili Crack'." He said he had gotten turned onto it a few months back and he and his friends had renamed it because it was so addictive it might as well be crack.

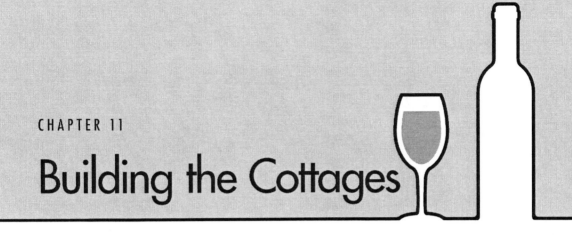

CHAPTER 11

Building the Cottages

The opportunity to build our five luxury cottages was the first real chance I had to put my stamp on the style and comfort of the Inn. Other than turning into a three-year project that ran $1 million over budget I think they turned out great! Though my partners were behind the project from the beginning, dealing with the neighbors and the County proved to be a lesson in accepting the absurd as other people's reality.

The concept was simple, we still had a little land we could build on, some of it right down in the vineyards, but we didn't want to get too big. Both we and the guests seemed to love the smallness of the Inn and though we could have fit much larger buildings on the land we had

available we didn't want to change the nature of the hospitality we had built. So five individual 800-square-foot cottages is what seemed to fit. Now to get the County and my neighbors to agree to the plan.

First, I should explain that in Napa County both the residents and the local governments are extremely protective of their agriculture, as well we need to be. Back in 1968 the County supervisors passed what was at the time the most restrictive land ordinance in the nation to limit the ability to subdivide agricultural land into building lots. This Agricultural Preserve ordinance has now been copied by many other communities and has been strengthened but never weakened from its original form. Great swaths of land outside of the various city limits of the towns in Napa County cannot be divided in anything smaller than 40 acre parcels and upon that 40 acres only one single family dwelling can be built. I could go on and on about the incredible benefits of this ordinance but the only real relevance it has to this story is that the property the Inn is built on is surrounded by land that falls under these restrictions and if it ever comes to a conflict between commercial development and agricultural protection, agricultural protection wins. And then there was archeological heritage, traffic mitigation, retail restrictions, sewer restrictions, rain run-off mitigation (which ended up costing $500,000 alone) and so many other demands of County micro-management that any sane person would have just given up. But eventually I waded through a couple years of hearings and briefs and negotiations that we finally got our permits to build.

One of the most amusing stories was the one about the need for an archeologist on site during the installation of a drainage culvert that now needed to be constructed down the entire length of the property. It turned out that even though we had already done extensive construction through most of this area there was a new sensitivity to our Native American heritage and there is no doubt the little knoll the Inn is built on is a sensitive area. For years I have told the story about the mountain (hill really) that is a big part of the Inn's view. When you look off to the east from almost any of our rooms, past the expanse of vineyards is a view of Glass Mountain. It is called Glass Mountain because it is virtually a mountain of obsidian. Right next to the site the Inn is built on is the ancient site of an Indian village that dates way back. There is evidence that tribes from all over the Western United States used to trek to Napa Valley for the high quality arrowheads that were produced right on the Inn's property and if you know what to look for and look carefully there are artifacts scattered all over the area. Now you need to know that I am a dyed-in-the-wool typical California liberal Democrat and when these issues first came up I was not only sympathetic but curious and excited about prospect of helping preserve this historical site.

My first meeting with the archeologist was fascinating. Walking around the south stretch of our property within moments he was pointing out obsidian flakes that were plainly (to him) leftover debris from the production of arrowheads, he found the stone base of a mortar and pestle in the stone wall that separates the Inn's property from our neighbor to the west and one arrowhead that was fairly intact. All of this he carefully replaced where he had found it and instructed me to always do the same.

Huh? I thought. We continued to tour the property and he continued to point out little shards of obsidian and explain how he was going to post one of his associates on-site while the digging of this 300 yard drainage ditch commenced. I was becoming less fascinated with every step we took.

"So what happens to all this stuff when we find it?" I finally asked.

"Well it depends on what we find," he replied. "Most everything we find we will just leave in place. We have warehouses full of these artifacts, in fact I was hoping you would want some. You could build a display, looking out towards Glass Mountain for your guests to get a true appreciation of the history of the area!"

"You have warehouses full of this stuff?"

"Sure."

"That no one sees? Just sitting there?"

"Yeah, it's a shame."

"And how much is this going to cost me?"

"Well," he started to see he might have just lost me. "We'll be using one of our lower cost associates (read undergrad student). We only charge $40 per hour (in 1999) for her."

So when construction finally started I had a young lady parked on our driveway in the general vicinity of the backhoe sleeping or reading in her car at $40 per hour for about a month. Surprisingly she didn't find any new artifacts, nothing to preserve or take back to the warehouse for no one to see.

Building these cottages to blend in with what we had built twenty-five years earlier was as big of a challenge as the constructing the original buildings. Some of the building materials were still simply not available. For instance the cornerstones and wall caps had been handmade and hand chiseled by my crew and me back in 1974. It turned out we were going to have to do that again if we wanted the same look. Before long we had a "brick factory" on the site cranking out rows and rows of handcrafted "stones" for the stone foundations and walkway corner pillars.

Stone walls started going up everywhere.

Me laying brick pavers.

And we started experimenting with there really cool paving bricks that we would end up becoming a defining look for the whole property.

With the end result turning out like this.

CHAPTER 12

More Stories from the Early Days

One of my favorite stories comes from back when we used to hire a lot of high school kids. I think the truth was that I was in my mid-twenties and didn't really want to supervise a bunch of people that were older than me.

One of the jobs we had back then was for a young man to head up to the Inn directly after school and build the fires in the fifteen rooms that had fireplaces. It was Steve's first day on the job. I was waiting for him and for a half hour or so I regaled him with all my vast knowledge of how to build a good fire. Start with the crumpled up newspaper, but make sure you separate every sheet of paper so that each clump of paper has good ventilation. Build a little log cabin with the kindling wood, again making sure there was space between each piece because fire just doesn't burn without air. Then place your two base logs on, making sure the split side is on the inside and the nice looking bark is facing the guest. Now the most important part, place the third log slightly askew on top of the other two logs. You need what? Yes, ventilation, but you also need to keep the heat from that initial kindling fire inside this chamber you just made to catch this nice oak wood properly. I then showed him around the property, where the supplies were, where the rooms that had fireplaces were, etc.

He was a friend of my younger brother's and I was known from time to time to help them score some beer so he put up with my detailed and laborious instructions. I then sent him off with a master key and a wood tote with one final instruction, "always knock at least three times and announce yourself loudly before entering a room".

I personally only know the end result of this story but here is the story my brother was able to glean from Steve a couple days later.

"I was on my third or fourth room when I headed over to the Brandy Barn. I found Room 22 which was on my list and knocked on the door — three times!

"Fireboy," I said. "Fireboy, I repeated two more times as I knocked and then inserted my key. I didn't even get into the room. There they were! Two bodies on top of all the covers, going at it. I stammered, 'I'm here to build your fire'. The guy looked up without skipping a beat. 'Go for it,' he said."

I looked at my brother. I might have been ten years older, but he knew me. "Of course," my brother responded without me having to ask, "I asked him why he quit!"

Another of my favorites is about my son Mike. It was a Saturday morning and there was trouble at the Inn. Someone had called in sick and I was needed to pull the shift. As a bit of a prank and probably because I was feeling a bit abused that my Saturday had just been mightily disrupted I barged into my son's room and announced

Mike at 12 or 13

that *we* had to go to work. I think he was 13 and though he had been around the Inn all his life I had never asked him to do any work around the place. He obviously tried to stuff the pillow over his head and ignore me but I wouldn't go away.

"Come on, we gotta go," I demanded.

Finally he dragged himself out of bed, threw on some clothes and followed me out the door. "What am I going to do?" he whined.

"You're going to help me check rooms, check-in guests, whatever it takes," I responded.

"OK," he kind of agreed and kind of didn't believe me.

I gave him some rudimentary training and explained to the guests he was dealing with that this was his first day on the job so go easy, and they did, and he did, and we got through the day with little strife and a little fun. The next morning he was still in bed at 10 (as every teenager wants to be) and I went in to check on him. He was lying in bed with a contemplative look on his face. "Dad," he said, "I'm the only one of my friends that has a job."

I was floored, but certainly couldn't show it. "Cool," I commented walking out the door. "We'll have to get you some more training."

"Cool," he said. He worked hard and well for the Inn all through high school, went off to college to get a degree in Hospitality Management and is now climbing the corporate ladder with his next step likely the General Manager of a 200 or 300 room property.

Equal time. Here's one about my daughter Kelly. As I mentioned in an earlier chapter a big part of the Inn's view, past the expanse of vineyards is of Glass Mountain, a mountain of obsidian.

We didn't really know this at the time, but we did know that the Hourglass vineyard that was just up the driveway on my parents' property was littered with obsidian. My little family lived in a small cottage on the property at the time and my daughter loved to go up into the vineyards to collect obsidian. She had a few boxes cluttering her room filled with the stuff and when I asked her what she was going to do with it (her room was quite small and the boxes were definitely in the way). "I'm going to sell it," she replied with confidence.

"Cool," was apparently my standard comeback.

The next weekend this little four-year-old was sitting on the stone wall at the front door of the Inn. "Mister," she would inquire of the arriving guests. "Do you want to buy some omsimium," and she would show them her wares. She was

Kelly at about 4 years old

so damn cute and so damn proud of her product, even though she couldn't pronounce it, I don't think there was a guest that walked by that didn't drop a buck or five on a couple rocks they would likely leave in their room.

About ten years later Kelly was now 13 or 14. My mother and I were in the middle of redesigning the bathrooms in the Main Building. We were no longer satisfied with the fiberglass shower stalls or linoleum bathroom floors that had seemed appropriate when our rates were around $50 per night, but now that they had tripled (over 20 years) we felt the guests deserved (and expected) more. We had already decided on the tiles for the showers and bath enclosures so now it was time to pick the floor tiles and cultured marble for the vanities. Since each of our rooms has its own color scheme we were pretty much forced to choose different floor tiles for each room. My mother and I had blocked out an entire afternoon to go room by room to get this job done. I guess it was in the summer because Kelly asked if she could come along. I said sure instead of, "do you really know what you're getting yourself into?" She had no idea how heated these "discussions" could get with my mother. My mother always picked THE most expensive option and THE most impractical from a maintenance/operational standpoint. Within an hour or so Kelly figured it out after Mom needed to "go get an ice tea".

Standing in the vanity of Room 6 Kelly seemed nonplussed. She started looking over the floor tile options since so far she had been relegated to looking over one of our shoulders. "I really like this combination," she said pointing to one of the more neutral squares with a smaller blue accent tile.

I looked at her choice and then at her, "I like it, but if you want to weigh in it'd be up to you to tell your grandmother."

"Okay," she shrugged. I assumed she didn't really grasp the severity of the potential reaction. After all, my mother is an amazing artist with a very developed esthetic, something she was quite convinced I didn't possess, let alone her thirteen-year-old granddaughter.

When Gramma came back with her iced tea Kelly launched right in, no preamble, no hesitation, just, "Gramma, I like this one."

My mom took the board from her without comment and reviewed the choices for a couple minutes, Kelly and I stealing glances at each other. "You know Kelly, I really like that one, too."

Excellent, was my only reaction at that moment, one down thirteen to go. Within an hour I realized I would be out voted 2 to 1 (if I even got a vote) so I just went back to my office. Every one of the tiles Kelly picked out first ended up being the final choice. I think that experience had a profound influence on Kelly (and my mom and me) because ten years later Kelly would have a degree in Interior Design and make her way back to the Inn to start redoing rooms with a decidedly younger eye than ever before.

I think the toughest task in those early days was trying to draw proper boundaries with the staff and various family members and develop policies that seemed fair, flexible to individual needs and compassionate. And as I have explained, everything was a wild mix. Not only did we have direct family members, but we had uncles and aunts, mothers and their children, even grandparents. We also had best friends (at one point it seemed we had the entire St. Helena High School girls' volleyball team working for us and when each year they made it to the play-offs — well — those were interesting weekends to get breakfast out and the rooms cleaned). We even had one of my former high school teacher's daughter working for me and I can tell you he did not like it when I tried to pull rank on him. OMG it could be a mess!!

Policies that came out of those days were things like:

- Male employees cannot wear make-up to work.
- Underwear cannot be worn as outerwear (it was the 80s after all).
- If you call in sick you must be available by phone AT HOME through the evening of that day (obviously this policy no longer works with cell phones).

- All major body parts must be covered from just below the shoulders to mid-thigh (I have never felt uniforms were appropriate for the atmosphere I am trying to create so we have had to come up with compromises).
- No family fights on WCI property! Leave it in the parking lot or take it home.

I was shocked when I went over to a staff member's house for a staff party (the very first year of Saturday Night Live) and found a brand new full set of WCI towels hanging in her bathroom. She hadn't even thought to hide them.

———————————

Here's another great story I had almost forgotten about. I don't remember her name, but I think she worked the breakfast shift. I was probably 24 at this point and she was probably 30. A nice, soft-spoken woman with a very gentle spirit. She came to me one day and said she wanted to throw a staff pool party. She said the house she was renting had a great pool and BBQ and if everyone brought a little something we could have it after most people got off for the day and party on into the evening. This was not at all unusual, we had a lot of parties back in those days. I put my stamp of approval on it and the word went out. On the appointed day my wife and I got there after my shift and there were fifteen or so people there already, but the party seemed somehow subdued. I think it was Kathleen who spotted us first and ran over.

"This is kinda awkward," she blurted, seemingly quite nervous.

"What?" I asked, still not oriented. But I didn't have any time to adjust as our hostess approached, totally naked, with a tray of appetizers. She smiled her sweet smile, her demeanor calm and soft as she welcomed us with the tray of food and — well — her nakedness. My wife was extremely not happy and immediately assumed I had either arranged or at least approved this whole thing. I had done neither, but I was also completely at a loss as to how to handle it or explain to my wife (I never really tried to hide the fact that I was a horn-dog) that I had nothing to do with this. So I didn't. I took the high

road, accepted an appetizer, hauled my Safeway bag of burger and buns to the BBQ and acted as if everything was just fine. Our host was equally naked but neither of them ever pushed an agenda or even acknowledged anything was out of the ordinary and when the evening chill finally started coming on they donned robes. As I remember it was a fun evening until I got home.

Since a few of these stories were about Mike and Kelly when they were younger I'll include a recipe here that dates back to those days. I think I've mentioned a few times that I learned most of my cooking skills at San Francisco City College. A few years after graduating I got a divorce from Mike and Kelly's mom Nita and I had a 40/60 split for child custody. When I had my kids I really wanted to expose them to better cooking so I was constantly trying out what I will call more sophisticated meals than tradition "kid fare". Both kids really loved "Blue Box" Macaroni & Cheese but of course I thought I could do much better. Plus I didn't want to eat that crap. Whipping up a white sauce was no big deal and I always had a few leftover cheeses in the fridge from whatever "entertaining" I had been doing so, no big deal, just throw it all together and they could see how easy it was to eat a great meal not out of a box. Throw a little steamed broccoli on the plate with a garlic aioli? Wrong!! They hated my special mac & cheese. They hated my aioli. They hated my slaved over beef stew, my scrambled eggs with smoked salmon, my chutney chicken. Pretty much anything I wanted to eat they didn't and vis-a-versa. So I went on strike. I announced one day when I picked them up with their suitcases that they were on their own. I had enough milk and cold cereal so they wouldn't starve, but beyond that they could figure it out if they wanted something hot. They were probably six and nine at this point and Mike figured out the Blue Box pretty quick, but after a few weeks they were sick of mac & cheese and cold cereal and were ready to negotiate. Though they were still kids and I had to adjust my expectations they started branching out at least a little and we maintained a modest truce for the next ten or so years.

Adult Mac & Cheese

by Jim

INGREDIENTS

2 tbls butter

2 tbls flour

1 cup milk

2 cloves garlic, crushed

A few grains cayenne

Salt and pepper to taste

1 lb whatever fun cheeses you have in the fridge you want to use up

Some bowtie (or any other) macaroni

DIRECTIONS

1. Melt butter in a sauce pan.

2. Add flour and make a roux, cooking it until it is light toasty brown.

3. Add garlic and cook another 30 seconds or so.

4. Add milk (or ½ & ½ if you are being very decedent) slowly to the roux and heat until thickened and creamy.

5. Add cayenne, salt and pepper.

6. Add cheeses and while this sauce is maturing cook whatever pasta you have chosen.

7. When pasta is done and very well-drained add pasta to sauce and mix well.

Chicken Liver and Portobello Mushroom Pate

by Jim

Considering my statements above I want to make it clear that I wasn't a complete brute. I never tried to feed this recipe to my kids. I understand there are certain boundaries that just can't be crossed. Chicken livers, and at least for my kids, Portobello mushrooms would just never fly with them, still don't.

INGREDIENTS

1 lb chicken livers

1 medium Portobello
    mushroom, sliced

1 medium onion, diced

8 large cloves garlic, minced

½ cube butter

¼ cup port

½ tsp salt

¼ cup red wine

1 tbls ground black pepper

1 cup half & half

DIRECTIONS

1. Melt butter in sauce pan. Sauté onions until translucent (or use a couple heaping spoonfuls of those caramelized onions you now keep in your refrigerator). Add garlic and sauté for a minute. Add mushroom, chicken livers, red wine, port, black pepper and salt. Simmer until livers are cooked through and alcohol has mostly cooked off. Let cool for 15 or 20 minutes. Throw in food processor and blend as you add the half & half. Place in a serving bowl or individual ramekins and chill for several hours. Great with grilled crusty sourdough or toast points.

The black pepper and port are key to this recipe. When I developed this recipe I wanted the black pepper to really stand out as the solo spice. I had just gotten out of culinary training and felt that black pepper had been so taken for granted that it had been relegated to an essential but almost irrelevant spice. People used to live and die bringing this spice to our ancestors' tables and I wanted to give it its due respect!

CHAPTER 14

Marketing My Way

I think most people think of me as a funny guy. Since I was such a puny little kid growing up I avoided all sorts of difficult or potentially violent situations by making people laugh instead of swing. I like to have fun, even at the potential cost of not being PC. I am likely to take a chance at being funny. Maybe I got a little of that from my father, who as I think I mentioned, made the first tag line for the Inn "For A Little *Peace* In The Country." He also coined the acronym for the communal sewer company we share with a few of our neighbors. It is called the St. Helena Integrated Treatment Company, or SHIT Co for short.

There were a lot of people who questioned (and still question) my decision to ramp up the photography on the Inn's website. I mean, you go on pretty much every other hotel website and see the same stuff, you see the bedroom with the bed, the drapes, the carpet and a few pieces of furniture. You get a decent representation of what the room is going to look like, and in my opinion you get a general idea of what the hotel is going to be like overall. Well, The Wine Country Inn never was and hopefully never will be simply a bed, some drapes and a few pieces of furniture. Hopefully we have created something much more than that, but how do you communicate that with standard hotel photography?

Personally I think this does it. Is it PC? Well, not for some. Is it funny and different? Hell yes! Does it belong on a commercial website that is trying to sell rooms to a wide cross-section of people? All I know is that photos like this piloted us through some very successful years and they definitely created a buzz. Pretty much every innkeepers' convention I went to used my site as an example of how to use humor to create an interesting and engaging website. And, man, they were a lot of fun to cast and shoot!

So the way these shoots worked is that I would go on these modeling websites and start searching around for models

within close proximity that were willing to work for half cash and half lodging trade. I figured I had a commodity easily as valuable as they did. This narrowed the field quite a bit. The toughest part was getting male models to go along with the trade payment scenario. The ratio was probably 20 to 1 female models to male models so the male models were much harder to bargain with. So I started asking the female models if they had any male friends they could bring along to do couples shoots.

This is kind of a long set up for a fun story, but this scenario was problematic at best. It was amazing what kind of non-photogenic partners or friends these lovely young women would show up with.

Tattoos were huge, clothing selection was slim at best and attitude was sometimes insurmountable. So there was this one female model we had shot once before and when I put a "call" out on this website for models she contacted me to see if I wanted to use her again. I explained my predicament. I wanted couples in my shots, after all it is couples I am attempting to attract. She told me she could bring her boyfriend. He was a professional photographer and assured me he had no visible tattoos, could dress the part and was very sensitive to working in this kind of environment, so attitude would not be a problem.

The appointed day arrived and I had everything set: the photographer, shot lists, the props, rooms blocked out, working lunch arranged, everything. Lights, camera, action? The woman showed up at the agreed upon time, 10:00, with some guy who was definitely not the guy she had sent me pictures of. Good looking guy, but not the guy. Crap! What happened? Sasha explained that her boyfriend had refused to come at the last minute and that she had madly scrambled. She explained that she was a true professional and had no intention of

letting me down. She had finally called a dear friend who she had dated a few years back and had kept in touch with because he had really connected with her children (she had two) and she felt he fit the bill and she felt comfortable working with him.

I had to start from step one! Look? Tattoos? Clothes? Attitude? I needed wholesome but fun and sexy at the same time. Though the guy seemed to hit on all cylinders it took an hour to work through all that and now my timing schedule was way off. The sun was blasting through the windows of the room I wanted to shoot earlier. We punted, grabbed lights, tripods, huge totes of equipment and moved

to the next room, missing the morning shots I really wanted. Everything actually went really well, David was great and we got some good shots. I approached Sasha at the end of the day (a very long day). "I appreciate the work you put in here, but we didn't get the morning shots I need. I have a couple rooms for you. Can you guys stay the night and we'll get the other shots in the morning?"

I think you can all see what is coming. They stayed for the next day of shooting and a couple weeks later I get a call from Sasha, "I just thought I'd tell you that I went home from your photo shoot and broke up with my boyfriend. He had never really connected with my kids and — well — Dave is a wonderful guy." Sometimes things are just staring you in the face and you can't see them. Dave and Sasha are now married and have become regular guests at the Inn. They just celebrated their fifth wedding anniversary with us and plan to keep coming back to celebrate a connection that probably would not have happened without an innkeeper's propensity to have fun with his work.

Then there were just the plain no-shows. On more than one occasion we would have everything set, literally months of preparation, and yet again the male model just wouldn't show up. Shot lists go out the window, props are useless and Jim is standing there with four or five people waiting for direction. I guess I'll have to sit in with this twenty or thirty-something woman with me, a definitely non-model material in my fifties. Furniture, covers, camera angles, how can we hide Jim and still get the essence of the shot? Crap!

Make him a leg and foot model!

Or an arm model.

Anything to hide the fact that this is definitely a stand-in.

I still think these are fun and successful photos, but sadly with the advent of Expedia and Hotels.com and what I would call anonymous marketing (on-line shopping instead of people phoning a friend to see where they stayed and why) the need arose to be more universally acceptable and PC (read vanilla). In fact I found out recently there was one major company in the Valley who refused to refer guests to us, not because the shots were too sexy — which I think they objected to also — but because they depicted alcohol other than wine (even though the spirits depicted are from a Napa Valley company), but because some of the shots, specifically the first one in this chapter, did not seem to suggest drinking responsibly. Oh well, I guess you can't have too much fun and call it work!

PB&J Ribs

by Jim

I have never cooked these ribs for anything but a crowd, so I don't really have the proportions down for a single rack. For probably fifteen years these have been a command performance at the Inn's Christmas party and for many a Chill & Grill in our backyard even though I normally cook them in the oven, unless it is just too damn not. Any self-respecting rib cook is going to tell you that this recipe is not real "rib cooking" and I agree, but then these ribs have won more than their fair share of ribbons so …?–

INGREDIENTS

3 racks babyback pork ribs, cut into individual ribs

1 jar of your favorite BBQ sauce

1 jar of Roasted Raspberry Chipotle Sauce (from Costso)

¾ cup roasted garlic

¼ cup molasses

1 tbls tabasco sauce

¼ cup honey

DIRECTIONS

1. Preheat oven to 400 degrees.

2. In a food processor add BBQ sauce and roasted garlic. Whirl until smooth. Add the peanut butter and again whirl until smooth. After you have incorporated the peanut butter you can add the rest of the ingredients in any order, making sure to incorporate each ingredient as you go so the sauce remains smooth. Pour sauce into a bowl.

3. Now at this point you can make some decisions. I have marinated the ribs for up to a few days in the sauce, I have dipped them into the sauce then straight onto a cookie sheet covered with parchment paper and I have done everything in between. The marinated ribs seem to turn out about the same as the freshly dipped ribs so the choice is yours. Either way you want to coat each rib with the sauce, place them at least a half-inch away from each other on a covered cookie sheet and bake them until deeply browned, just an inch away from burnt, in a medium hot oven for about 40 minutes.

Roasted Red Bell Pepper Dip
by Diane

This is an incredibly popular dip that we have served during our evening wine service for over twenty years. We have made it with both jarred roasted red bell peppers and peppers from our own gardens and both are excellent.

INGREDIENTS

1 cup mayonnaise

½ cup sour cream

8 red bell peppers, roasted and seeded (1 large jar of roasted red peppers may be substituted)

1 or 2 roasted jalapeno If a little heat is desired

4 large cloves garlic, minced

2 tbls fresh basil

DIRECTIONS

1. Pat freshly roasted or jarred peppers until as dry as possible.

2. Place all ingredients in a food processor and pulse the blades to chop and blend peppers with the other ingredients a dozen or so times. The peppers should still be in small chunks, so don't over mix.

3. Chill for at least an hour before serving to allow flavors to marry and the dip to set up a bit.

This is the original recipe except the original called for dried basil and we grow so much basil I just couldn't go there. I also dry my own hot pepper flakes and I can't help throwing a palmful of those in either. This is a subtly flavored dip so it should be served with a neutral cracker. Surprising good on a Ritz.

Italian White Bean & pesto Dip

by Diane

INGREDIENTS

½ cup mayonnaise

1 16 oz garbanzo beans, drained

1 ½ tbls lemon juice

¼ tsp salt

2 heaping tbls pesto

DIRECTIONS

1. Place all ingredients except mayonnaise into a food processor and blend until smooth.

2. Add mayonnaise and plus until mixed.

3. Chill for 2 hours before serving.

CHAPTER 15

Problems with Guests and Townies

There is no doubt that folks have fun in our rooms (reminds me of the story of a single Innkeeper and his third date). Sometimes that stays quite private and sometimes this fun becomes a little more public.

Twenty or so years ago I had an idea to remodel our primary suite. At the time the door to Room 20 entered into a sitting room and then meandered into a bedroom that was basically the same size and configuration of a number of our other rooms. So basically the only difference between the suite and the smaller much less expensive rooms was a sitting room that I figured was seldom used by individual couples. Maybe, if two or more couples were traveling together it might be used a bit to entertain, but since the fireplace and a nice couch were in the bedroom, that's where I would spend my time. *And* bathrooms were becoming a real luxury amenity that was just not the case when the Inn was first built. So I decided to change the sitting room into a huge bathroom with a panoramic picture window overlooking the Valley, a luxurious two-person jetted tub, a large double vanity with heated mirrors that would never fog up, a 2-headed walk-in shower and heated tile floors. We then ripped out the original bathroom and expanded the bedroom to accommodate a much nicer sitting area in front of the fireplace and a king-sized bed. Wow! It turned out great if I do say so myself.

Our newly renovated suite opened to great fanfare and an enthusiastic reception by our guests. About a week after we opened it one of the housekeeper reported that the towel bar that was mounted below the deck of the vanity between the two sinks had come off. Maury, my Facilities Supervisor immediately went over and reattached it. About four days later the towel bar was off again, this time the screws were stripped from the wood. Puzzled, Maury went to the hardware store for bigger screws. A week later the bigger screws had proven

insufficient and the towel bar was laid neatly on the floor by yet another couple. I was called in at this point to solve the mystery of the troublesome towel bar. Over a three week period we had reattached the towel bar four times, with different couples staying in the room each time. After hearing the details and standing in my brand new sexy bathroom I walked up to where the towel bar should have been, bent over to hold onto it and looked up at Maury's reflection in the huge 8' by 5' mirror. He was simply not picturing what I was picturing until I waggled my butt at him.

"Oh God," he jolted, neither one of us really liking the visual I was displaying but suddenly appreciating it if it had been someone else. "We're going to have to find somewhere else for that towel bar," was his immediate reaction.

"Are you kidding me?!" I shot back. "We just have to come up with a better way of attaching

it!" That one little towel bar now has a massive support system that goes through the vanity and into the studs of the wall three feet away (all hidden in the cabinetry). And though we have had to replace the bar a few times over the years it's all money well spent.

Along that same line, while we were redoing this room (review the photo above) I asked our curtain supplier to come up and help us problem-solve the window treatment for the bathroom window. We needed some coverage, but we didn't want to diminish the view. There were still two carpenters working in the room when Maury and I showed this rather attractive woman into the bathroom.

Immediately she blurted, "This is the perfect place for a top-down bottom-up!!"

Not having a clue what she was talking about but also not missing the gutter humor involved in that statement I wisecracked. "My favorite," with a look over my shoulder at the other guys. They immediately started snickering but the woman went on nonplussed. "Exactly," she was thinking out loud. "It's a wide opening but I think it would be fine."

"Never too wide for a top-down bottom-up," I ventured. The guys behind me needed to head for the other room. Maury turned purple. Way too late I realized this woman could feel quite vulnerable if she caught on to the joke, we had just met after all. I stopped my wisecracking and eventually learned that a top-down bottom-up was a shade that can be raised from the bottom or lowered from the top.

As I think I've mentioned earlier, from 1977 up until November of 2013 we didn't have anyone on duty at the Inn from 10 p.m. until 8 a.m. We certainly had people on call for emergencies, but for the most part guests were on their own. This meant that the pool and hot tub were also left unsupervised and believe it or not unlocked all night long. I think many a guest enjoyed the privacy and seclusion of this amenity, especially on one of those nights where the skies are so clear the heavens look crusted with layer upon layer of stars. Unfortunately

When I asked her how she got around our security guard she came back laughing, "Oh, Bob? He doesn't actually get in the tub with us but I think he is pretty disappointed on the nights we don't show up." In the spirit of a dedicated innkeeper I stayed until the bar closed, invited the girl up to the hot tub and quietly had a little talk with Bob when he arrived.

the local townies are no dummies and neither are the local college kids from up at Pacific Union College (a private Seventh-day Adventist college).

The obvious solution was to hire a private security company to drive by three or four times a night to check up on things. But I would still get the occasional midnight call from a guest saying that there was too much noise coming from the pool area and I would have to drive up and boot kids out. One night when I was in my late 30s and single I was chatting this girl up at a local bar and when I told her what I did for a living she immediately started guiltily telling me about all the times she and her friends snuck into my hot tub.

So now without a security company (I tried two others that met with about the same results) I just kind of played it by ear. If I got called I would go and deal with it and if I didn't get called, no harm no foul. That is until the college kids started coming down en masse. On my wife's 40th birthday I surprised her by inviting four of her closest girlfriends and their husbands to stay at the Inn for the weekend. I had a full weekend planned and after dinner on Saturday night we all came back to the Inn with the plan of spending some time in the hot tub and pool. I guess we spent a bit of time in our rooms because sometime between the time we came home from dinner and we started walking down to the pool area about five cars had parked up the driveway by the pool (it turned out there were another five cars parked down on the main road) and at least 40 kids cavorting in the pool and hot tub. I was blown away. These guys were getting way to brazen. Indignantly, in my Wine Country Inn robe and swimming suit I marched into the area and started demanding everyone pack up and leave. They all just kind of looked at me and kept cavorting: cannonballs into the pool, playing grab-ass under the water, making out in the hot tub, my wife and friends looking at me as if to say 'really Jim, is this how it goes around here?'

Finally after yelling a couple more times for them to leave one of the kids approached me. "The owner is cool with us being here, we have permission," he said earnestly.

"I am the owner, and no it is not cool," I replied, rather heated at this point.

The young man was calm and staunchly insistent. "No really, you couldn't be. We have permission, it's all over school that we can come down whenever we want." The conversation went on for at least three or four minutes, me insisting I was the owner, him insisting I couldn't be. Being before everyone had a cell phone on them it finally ended with me, "Look, I'm going to go up to the office and call the Sherriff now so if you guys don't want to get arrested I suggest you get the hell out of here." Reluctantly the kids packed up and left. My first call Monday morning was to the Dean of Students at the college.

My call to the college slowed things down to a trickle, but the incursions still didn't stop. Finally I paid one of my staff to spend a few nights in one of the rooms overlooking the pool area and gave him instructions to call me if he observed any non-guest activity. Sure enough on his third night of observations he called me about 8:30 in the evening to say that there were kids down at the hot tub. I assured him that the pool was open to guests until 10 and these must be Inn guests enjoying the amenity they had paid for. He explained that he had watched two cars pull up the driveway from the road, park and traipse down to the pool area, laughing and calling out the whole way. He was a Hispanic man with not great English skills and informed me he was not about to go down and try to kick these kids out. I only live a few miles from the Inn so I headed up. Much to my surprise I found eight college kids (good Seventh-day Adventists mind you), four guys and four girls, casual as could be, enjoying the hot tub… buck naked. At 8:30 in the evening!! Primetime for paying guests to start showing up for an after-dinner soak. They didn't even have the courtesy to wait until their little escape would likely go unnoticed. I was flabbergasted!

"Wha? Wha? What do you think you are doing?" I finally chocked out my words. "It's 8:30!! Not only do you not belong here — you're naked! Are you begging me to call the Sheriff? Get out of here!"

"OK, mister," one of the girls whined as only an entitled twenty-something kid can do, "We'll go, but you gotta turn around." Not only did refuse to budge, but I think I mentioned something about adding indecent exposure to the charges of trespassing if they didn't grab their stuff and go without any more comments.

Things quieted down for a month or so as I remember, but soon enough I got another call, this time from a guest complaining about too much noise. I guess most of you are figuring I am an amazing softy at this point, but I was a kid once and I know what I would have done if this opportunity had been available when I was that age, so it took me a long time to finally call the Sherriff. So this time I pulled up the driveway and checked the cars out while I waited for the Sherriff to arrive. Sure enough the two cars had Pacific Union College parking permits. The Sherriff arrived and I briefed him before we went down to the hot tub. There were six of them this time (all with swimsuits on, thank God) none of whom I recognized from previous events. So, with very little fanfare they were all ticketed for trespassing and sent on their way home. A few of them were really scared when they were told that they would have to go to court and they would now have a police record. Their parents were not going to be pleased.

The next Monday I called the Sherriff who had responded to the call and told him I really didn't want these kids to end up with a record. I told him I had an idea; what if I contacted these kids and made them work off their crime by doing chores around the Inn for a couple weekends. He said he thought that was a great idea and gave me their names and phone numbers. I called all six of them to set a time and date when they needed to be in my office if they didn't want to go to court. I put on my sternest face and received the four of them who arrived on time. I asked where the other two were and they said one should be here shortly but the other one was traveling in Europe with her parents and would have her lawyer contact me. Well, la-tee-da.

I was in the middle of laying on my deal for them, 32 hours each of scrubbing pool tiles, polishing deck chairs and what-not for me to drop the charges, when the other kid came rushing in.

"Sorry I'm late," he started in, then kind of paused as he looked at me and then down at one of the portraits I have on my desk. "Is that? Yeah! That's my Aunt Lorinda!" looking at the picture of my wife on my desk.

"That is Lorinda alright, my wife," I wanted to laugh, but I was in the middle of doing my stern thing so I rallied, "And you think that is going to cut you some slack? I don't think so. You're late, sit down over there. You just added 8 hours to your sentence if you decide you don't want to go to court." Sheepishly he took his place and listened quietly to my terms. They all took the deal and the guys worked so hard and so well I ended hiring two of them to do more work around the place, for pay this time. My favorite part of the story was that the next weekend I attended a wedding on my wife's side of the family and her little nephew was the best man. His getting busted by me had made it all through the crowd and I must have had eight or so uncles, aunts, grandparents and family friends pull me aside and tell me to really stick it to him (mostly all in good fun). The only bad part is that the girl who was traveling in Europe ended up getting off scot-free. Apparently giving these kids a deal like that followed the spirit of the law but maybe not the letter of it.

Then there is the story I refer to only as The Naked Guy. I was getting ready to head up to the Inn one morning when I got a rather frantic call from the front desk saying they needed me right away. When I get a call like that things like shaving and brushing your teeth kind of go out the window. I headed up, coffee as a mouth wash (thankfully I don't use cream anymore) and hurried straight for the front desk. There were two couples waiting for me, both quite agitated.

"He didn't actually get in our room," one man started in with no preamble. "He was rattling our patio door and mumbling loudly, but I yelled at him and he went away."

The next guy started in, "I'm really near-sighted and a sound sleeper, but my wife woke up!"

I wanted to be respectful, but I was struggling here. I had no idea what these folks were talking about and I was not sure I wanted to know (but of course I had to). "Can we start at the beginning?"

"I think I was awake through the whole thing," one of the women volunteered. "We're staying in Room 4, on the ground floor just below." (We were in the front desk area, which is right above Room 4). "I woke up when this man (she pointed at the other couple) started yelling. He seemed quite agitated. Both our windows were open so I could hear him quite clearly. He was yelling at somebody not to come into his room." She took a couple breaths and waited to see if anyone wanted to add anything. "Then I hear someone rattling the handle of *our* door. I tried to wake my husband, but he's like the dead when he's asleep. So I just kinda froze. I am even more blind than my husband but I thought I saw the screen on the window come down and then I definitely saw a shape — a man — crawling through our window. Honey, honey, you gotta wake up. There's somebody in our room — and I think he's naked."

Her husband finally pipes in, "My wife finally succeeded in waking me up. I could hear her kinda loud whispering to me and I could hear the guy in the room next door yelling 'Don't come back over here.' I was completely disoriented and more than a little panicked while I was hunting around for my glasses, the whole time my wife is urgently whispering 'He's right there, in the corner, trying to pretend like he's a plant or something.' I finally find my glasses and throw them on my face and sure enough, in the corner of our room is this guy, naked and cowering like if he doesn't move I won't notice him. I start yelling at him to get the hell out of my room and then I hear this gentleman," he points at the couple standing beside him, "yelling 'don't send him back over here.' Finally the guy climbs back out the window and that's the last I see of him. We checked our room and nothing was missing except a t-shirt we were letting dry out on our patio."

My desk clerk then pipes in, "They described the man for me, I'm almost certain it is the man staying up in Room 14."

Obviously I apologize profusely to the guests from both rooms and tell them we will be comping both of their stays. Then I call the Sherriff, the whole time dreading the idea of spotting this guy before the cops arrive. But I don't and the Sherriff gets there, strutting in through the Common Room filled with guests who are really not thinking this is the kind of place that would need a Sherriff's attention. After full explanations we head up to Room 14 and knock on the door. No answer. We knock a few more times and finally I get my master key out and we go in. The guests are gone but all their stuff is still strewn all over the room (they were scheduled to stay for another night) including the missing t-shirt from Room 4's patio. It's obvious we have the right guy and though we give the Sherriff the guy's license plate number neither of us are very confident these guys will be spotted out on the streets. So the Sherriff puts a little note on the back of one of his business cards to call him and tapes the card to the outside of the room door. My staff and I wait around all day, antsy about how this is all going to shake out. About 4 in the afternoon a bewildered woman steps up to the front desk wondering what that note was on their door and why her boyfriend bolted without explanation, leaving her stranded here with no car and no way to get home. Feeling sorry for the woman I proceeded to give her the highlights of her boyfriend's midnight adventures. After absorbing this information for a little bit she explained how her boyfriend and she had been up all night drinking and at some point he had gone downstairs to get a soda. She admitted that she had been quite toasted at that point and though she had thought he had been gone for an inordinate amount of time she had been fading in and out by then so she didn't really question him when he returned.

None of this was really making a whole lot of sense to me so I kept pressing this young lady. The Sherriff needed to talk to her boyfriend and we needed to settle up a mounting bill for the money we were out for the rooms we had comped, not to mention the room she was still in. The phone number her boyfriend had given us was some office in San Jose that was closed for the weekend so that was a dead end, too. Finally, the girl pulled me aside, "I know this guy is good for it. He's some big wig in the Silicon Valley, but I really can't be of much help. This 'date' we were on was arranged through a website I advertise on. I really don't have any better contacts for this guy than you do."

At this point it was getting on into the evening and can you believe the Sherriff informed me that it would actually be illegal for me to evict this lady at this hour. Since we are out in the country, there is no cab service in the area and no hotels within walking distance it was illegal to put someone out on the street, even though this particular lady had most likely walked many a street. So we let her stay and somehow by morning she was gone.

Fortunately the guy had actually registered under his own name and the phone number he had given was real because Monday morning I was talking to this guy at his office. He was *extremely* cooperative and *extremely* interested in how we could make this all go away so when I mentioned the amount the Inn was out for all our comping and inconvenience he assured me we would have a check in the mail within the next couple of days. Sure enough, two days later I got a nice fat cashier's check for the full amount I had asked for.

》———————《

Just recently we had a real doozy. Kelly, my daughter, was working the front desk when she got a phone call from a guest who was due to arrive later in the day.

"My boyfriend won't get in the car!" the woman was shouting over the phone before my daughter could even get her Good Morning greeting out of her mouth. "He is refusing to get in the car!"

Thinking something must be terribly wrong my daughter immediately goes into hyper-help-the-guest mode. "Are you safe?"

"We're at the airport!" the woman screams back, "and he won't get in the f'n car — it's only a town car. He thought I had ordered a limo. Can somebody come pick us up?"

Now I have to tell you, my daughter is about the most customer service-orientated person I know and she loves the Inn as an integrated piece of her soul, but I can just see her eyes flying open and her jaw dropping. "Ah — well — we don't have a car that can do that. I could make some calls but it would take anyone from up here a couple hours to get to you. Did we arrange this transportation for you?" thinking the woman on the other end of the phone was possibly blaming us for this snafu.

"No, no, no! But it's a town car! The driver says we need a limo to have our drinks on the way up!"

My daughter's sympathy and hyper-service mode suddenly flew out the window and her WTF bullshit meter took its place. "I can give you the numbers of a few local limo services if you'd like, but I would talk to the driver and see if his company can't send a different car." All the while thinking 'Oh boy, these folks are going to be fun'.

Though the woman continued to try to get Kelly to help her, the long and short was that beyond giving her two numbers for local limo companies there was little else we could do for them. About two hour later a beat up Oakland city cab pulled up in front of the Inn (a first) and two passengers literally fell out of the back seat, the woman struggling to make it to the rock wall that surrounds our landscaping and that was as far as she could make it. The man held onto the door of the cab and was finally able to navigate his hand to his wallet and throw four hundred dollar bills at the driver who was removing their luggage from the trunk. After pocketing the money (apparently the agreed upon price because the cabbie made no attempt to give him change) the driver pulled something else out of the trunk and walked off a few feet towards some parked cars. He oriented himself and laid out his prayer rug. As my staff was assessing the condition of our wonderful new guests the driver knelt down and prayed, right there in the parking lot, for more than a few minutes. By this time the man was haranguing the woman, dropping F-bombs and C-bombs as she tried to concentrate on the spinning bricks at her feet. There were now three of my staff on scene trying to contain the situation. My daughter thought she had better check on the cab driver.

When the cabbie was done she asked if he was alright. "Oh, they were fine to me," he revealed, "but the words that came out of their mouths to each other — I am not allowed to listen to such language." He announced as he was folding his rug. "I will have to pray more, but I would like to leave now."

"Of course, of course," my daughter backed out of his direct line to the driver's door. The cab was gone in moments and my staff was encouraging our new guest to quiet down. The woman had still not moved. We assessed that the man was now under control enough to go inside to check in so one of my staff stayed with the woman while the man came inside to do the formalities. By the time he was done checking in the woman seemed to have recovered enough to walk to her room. Fortunately they had booked one of our vineyard cottages so even if they decided to get rowdy again they would be relatively isolated. My front desk staffer (who wants to remain anonymous) showed them to their room, their luggage would follow. Immediately upon entering the room the man started up again, but this time he included my staffer. He started describing what he was going to have his girlfriend to do to him in the most graphic language possible and was waving a hundred bill at my staffer to stay and watch. "She loves it, trust me." The woman then came to life from her place sprawled on the couch, joined her boyfriend by approaching my staffer seductively, all hands and pouty eyes and murmurs. My staffer made it back to the Front Desk literally shaking.

When the Sherriff's deputies arrived (two decided to come on this call) I brought them and my staffer out to my office. My staffer proceeded to tell the whole story but at the end insisted on not pressing charges. I insisted that I wanted them out of my hotel, but the Sherriff explained that if my staff was not willing to press charges and the guests stayed in their room until they were sober there was little they could do beyond having a little chat with them. By the time we got to their room the woman was passed out in the bed and the guy seemed quite calm and rational. We had a long chat laying out the ground rules for them to be able to make it through the weekend without spending most of it in jail. With the exception of finding three or four empty vodka bottles in bushes throughout the landscaping we had no further incidents, partly because I insisted that no one on the staff approach them or their cottage alone.

Sometimes you just have to shake your head at the gall of some people. Just a few weeks ago I was working at the front desk when the phone rang. I picked it up and gave my normal greeting.

"Oh good," the woman launched, "I was hoping to speak to the owner or the manager."

"How can I help you?" It is seldom good when a conversation starts like this, but hey, if I can solve a problem before it gets any bigger all the better.

"I have a request and I know it is going to sound strange, but I just don't know what else to do," she sounded just a little sheepish.

"Sure," I said, practicing my active listening.

"I have a gift certificate for an inn down the road (she used the name of the inn, but I won't here). The inn has closed and — well — we want to come up this weekend but I can't seem to get my money back from the former innkeeper."

"OK," my active listening was getting a little muddled.

"I've talked to the gentleman three times now and each time he says he will send me the money, but I haven't received it."

She went on a bit more, but I was still unclear why she had called me.

Finally I thought I would break in. "I wasn't aware that inn had closed and I never did meet the new owner. He had just bought it a couple years ago so this surprises me a bit," thinking the woman was going to ask me to somehow intervene.

"It's our fourteenth wedding anniversary this weekend," she went on unfazed. Then she got down to it, "I was hoping you would honor my gift certificate."

"Wha?" was about all I got out before she kept going, now maybe just a little tearful.

"I just don't know what else to do. We can't afford to vacation as it is and now to be out this money! And it's our anniversary."

"I'm sorry," I stammered, thinking to myself this is quite possibly the most ballsy request I have ever heard. "We are almost full for this weekend. I certainly see that you are in a tough spot, but — well — I guess I could give you a bit of a discount, but I have no way of collecting on your gift certificate."

"No, I understand," she admitted. "But I see on your website that you're not full. It's our anniversary and I was just hoping — "

I hadn't even looked at our booking screen yet so apparently she knew more than I did what our availability was, though that was hardly the point. I now looked and concluded we likely would not fill up, but I wasn't about to just give her a room for free. "You want to come up for two nights?" I asked.

"Yes, for the weekend," she stated.

"I feel badly for your situation," I let that sink in for a moment, "but the best I can do is a 20 percent discount. I have one of our least expensive rooms open," and quoted her the price with this substantial discount.

"Oh," disappointment dripping from her voice. I let it drip. Silence. Drip.

Something came over me, "Tell you what," I said, "If you can come up Saturday and Sunday I can let you stay Sunday at no charge. We won't be full Sunday."

"Oh," zero acknowledgement of my unbelievable generosity. My mouth dropped along with any further sympathy.

I was now trying to figure out how I could back out of even the offer for a 20 percent discount.

"Do you know any other hotel I could call that might help me?" somehow this lady was convinced that somebody other than the out-of-business innkeeper down the road owed her something.

"Honestly," I was floored and done. "This is one of the most bizarre conversations I have ever had. I am a pretty soft-hearted guy, but no, I can't imagine any other hotel even listening to your story as long as I have." When silence continued on the other end. "There really isn't anything else I can do. I will stick to my offer but that is it, I simply won't give you any more."

"This really doesn't work for me," she responded. "I'll have to check with my husband."

At this point my daughter Kelly had heard the last part of my side of the conversation and was standing over my shoulder listening. "I'll tell my daughter about this offer, so if you call back, ask for Kelly." I hung up.

I think you're guessing this was not the end of it. I sheepishly told Kelly what I had done and that I was hoping we wouldn't hear from her again. Not so lucky.

The next day I get a call from my daughter. Not only has the woman booked for Friday and Saturday nights but she has followed it up with a list of special wineries she wants us to get her into, you guessed it, for free. My daughter explained that she was now on her fourth email to the woman quoting the prices of the different special tours she was requesting and explaining that she would need her permission to give her credit card information to these wineries to hold these reservations. "Who is this woman?" my daughter demanded.

"A major P-I-A," was all I could say. "Thanks for taking one for the team."

The woman showed up on Friday afternoon and immediately searched Kelly out. Excited she asked, "OK, what were you able to set up for us?"

"Ah, nothing," my daughter responded, sure there were going to be fireworks from the woman. "You never gave me permission to use your credit card to reserve the reservations."

"Well that's ridiculous," the woman started in, her husband standing back. "Why would they need …" were the first four words of the next four hundred that repeatedly called into question my daughter's skills as a super concierge.

My daughter finally got the chance to check them in and headed back to the front desk to count to one hundred. Sure enough she doesn't get to thirty-five before the woman is back at the front desk. "This room won't do," she explains. "My husband needs a balcony."

"Yes Ma'am," Kelly smiled, "I happen to still have a room with a balcony available. Let me check the rate on that room." She gave her the rate with no discount (atta girl).

The woman's eyes flew wide. "Can I see pictures of it?" she asked.

Kelly brought up our website and showed her the room. "Oh, no, no, that won't do," the woman moans sadly. "The balcony is covered, my husband needs more air. Before we arrived I went on-line and noticed one of your cottages is still open, we'll take that."

"Absolutely," Kelly returned, "the rate on that cottage is $795." Kelly would have given it to anyone off the street for $575 this late in the day, but that wasn't happening.

"We use TripAdvisor a lot," the woman came back, "and you are not being very accommodating."

The conversation was over, we draw the line at blackmail. Kelly told the woman in no uncertain terms that there was nothing further we could do for her and excused herself. Sure enough, before the woman had even checked out she had left a scathing review on TripAdvisor. And sure enough, before the week was out we had gotten it removed. TripAdvisor doesn't appreciate blackmail either.

Rubbed and Pan Seared Salmon
inspired by Deniese

INGREDIENTS

3 serving-sized salmon steaks

2 tbls clarified garlic butter

The Rub

1 tsp Spanish paprika

1 tsp grey salt

1 tsp black pepper

1 tsp fennel

1 tsp garlic powder

1 tsp dried dill

¼ tsp cayenne pepper

1 tsp dried mustard

1 tsp marjoram

1 tsp dried parsley

DIRECTIONS

1. Make rub ahead of time and store in an air tight container.

2. A couple hours or so before cooking remove steaks from refrigerator and rub thoroughly with spice mixture. Return to refrigerator while making sauce below. Let both rest in refrigerator until ready to cook.

3. Heat clarified butter in a heavy skillet until almost smoking. Add salmon and sear until nutty brown on first side. Flip and sear other side for 30 seconds or so.

4. Plate immediately and drizzle with any remaining clarified butter and garnish with a large dollop of Red Pepper Aioli.

Red Pepper Aioli
by Deniese

INGREDIENTS

2 cups mayonnaise

3 cloves garlic

Juice from ½ lemon

½ tsp cayenne pepper

1 roasted red bell pepper

4 green onions, chopped, just
the greens

Salt and pepper to taste

DIRECTIONS

1. Place all ingredients except mayonnaise into food processor and blend until smooth. Add mayonnaise and pulse until blended.

2. Refrigerate for at least an hour before serving.

Goes great with the salmon recipe above or fresh Dungeness crab. Also is an excellent dip on a vege tray which is how we usually use it at the Inn.

Zucchini Mushroom Frittata
by Doris

INGREDIENTS

3 medium zucchini, sliced

2 bell peppers, diced

2 cloves garlic, minced

12 eggs

16 oz cream cheese, softened with fork

4 cups stale or oven dried sourdough, cubed

3 cups shedder cheese, shredded

1 lb mushrooms

1 onion, diced

4 tsp olive oil

½ cup cream or ½ & ½

Salt and pepper to tastes

DIRECTIONS

1. Remove cream cheese a few hours before starting (the night before if you are preparing this recipe first thing in the morning).

2. Preheat oven to 325 degrees.

3. Sauté zucchini, mushrooms, bell pepper, onion and garlic in olive oil until soft. In a large bowl beat eggs and cream.

4. Add softened cream cheese and incorporate.

5. Add cheddar cheese, bread, vegie mixture, salt and pepper and mix well. Pour into large greased baking dish.

6. Bake for 30 minutes or until firm in the center.

Winter Mash

by Lorinda

Now I love me some mashed potatoes, but for a dinner party my wife and I like to shake it up a bit. So along with the Beef Bourguignon recipe I gave you earlier this is a fun alternative.

INGREDIENTS

A palmful of Kosher salt

1 lb russet potatoes, peeled

1 medium turnip, peeled

1 medium parsnip, peeled

3 or 4 medium carrots, peeled

5 to 8 cloves garlic, peeled

¼ cup milk

½ cup buttermilk

½ stick butter

A few good shakes
    Worcestershire Sauce

¼ tsp paprika

Salt and pepper to taste

DIRECTIONS

1. Cut all veggies into roughly equal sized pieces of about an inch square. Place Kosher salt and all veges in a large pot and cover with water. Place pot on medium heat and bring to a boil. Simmer until all veges are fork tender.

2. Heat both milks and butter in the microwave until milks are warm and butter is melted (but don't boil). Heating the milk is a step I see a lot of folks skip, but this step is not just to keep the mash hot, it is to sweeten the milk slightly.

3. Drain veggies and reserve liquid. Add Worcestershire Sauce and paprika. Mash the veggies with whatever implement you prefer (my wife using an electric mixer, but I prefer either a ricer or an old fashioned hand masher) while slowly adding milk mixture until you attain the consistency you desire. Salt and pepper to taste.

I just can't throw the cooking liquid away. If I have time I will reduce it down and add it to whatever sauce I am making, being sure it is not too salty, but it usually isn't.

CHAPTER 16

Much Ado About Bacon (and Fritos?)

During my culinary training our instructors insisted on referring to bacon as a condiment, an ingredient or a garnish but not as anything beyond that, not even a side dish. Personally I think that is an insult to this most revered meat. For years I have gone to innkeeping meetings and conventions where some new innkeeper will tell a story we have all heard, but we never tire of. They will have a guest that, for dinner insists they are vegetarian and insist on the most minute detail of their diet be catered to: a separate pan to cook their spinach in that has never seen animal fat; mashed potatoes made without butter or milk; salt be removed from their table. Then in the morning these very

same guests are going back to the buffet line for a second helping of crispy, fatty, salty bacon. Europeans still marvel at this delicacy of crispy bacon even though I can't imagine they can't now get it in their home country.

There's no doubt about it, bacon has a special place in most of our hearts (and arteries). Even my wife's. I have to tell you this story that occurred about a year and a half ago. My wife and I were headed down to Napa to meet up with some friends for dinner. We had actually gotten out of the house a little early so we decided to stop by Press, St. Helena's premiere steak house, for a relaxing drink after a stressful week (I hope I have by now convinced you that innkeeping can actually be stressful sometimes). We were seated at the bar and my wife was glancing at the bar menu, more out of habit than with any idea that she was going to order anything. She started laughing and pointed out to me that this particular menu was devoted strictly to bacon. Bacon? Bacon only? We were both intrigued and a little confused. We had never seen anything like this before. Along with that, my wife was raised as a vegetarian and thinks that my weekend tradition of including crispy bacon in pretty much anything we come up with for breakfast as more than a little obsessive. We got the bartender's attention and she explained how the chef had searched out artisanal bacons for all over the United States and this was his way of offering these delicacies as kind of an educational experience. There were seven different bacons and they could be ordered individually or as a sampler plate. My wife was a bit grossed out thinking that she could barely stand the idea of all that fat once or twice a week for breakfast, but to add it to an evening meal that is also likely to

be packed with way too many calories, well that was just laughable. That is until the aromas of a sampler plate started drifting over to us from the two guys sitting next to us that had no such aversion. My wife didn't even look at me to see what I wanted to do, she just waved down the bartender and order up our own sampler plate. Since then I have told pretty much every guest I run into that has plans to eat at Press that this is a must. It was one of the most interesting taste experiences I have had in a very long time.

»———————————«

Chef Ryan is a bit of a nut about bacon too. Bacon has never been a part of our buffet at the Inn, at least until Ryan came along. Now we have a few recipes for different bacons and return guests salivating upon check-in with their first questions having to do with the menu for the next morning's breakfast. There is no doubt Chef Ryan has created a bit of a monster.

As I mentioned earlier in this story, about a year ago Chef came up with another innovation, Bacon Pop Corn.

As you are all probably aware, the Inn hosts an evening appetizer spread along with a local winery who hosts a tasting of their wines with the food. It is quite a spread with veggies from our gardens, various other crudité, nice cheeses, at least two of the dips written up in this book, an interesting dipping oil with our homemade bread and at least one hot appetizer. One day, in addition to all these other goodies, Ryan brings out a bowl of popcorn. Now, the Wine Country Inn is a casual place. I have worked all my life to create an atmosphere of comfort and ease, but popcorn!!? Our food is purposefully not high-brow but that doesn't mean we don't take it seriously. It takes a lot of back-of-the-house work to make everything look so effortless. Ryan could probably see my reaction yet he just smiled and suggested I give it a try. Since there were guests all around I had little choice, I took a few kernels and plopped them in my mouth. Man was that good! I could taste the bacon right off the bat. He quickly explained that this was his new creation, he had fried up a little bacon and actually popped the popcorn in the

Chef Ryan with his Hot Sweet Bacon

bacon grease. Then he had chopped up the bacon, sprinkled the popped corn with some spices and the chopped bacon, what did I think?

Not only did I love it, but the guests who were there that day devoured it. Though I give Chef full credit for this recipe it was too good not to steal. A week or so later I decided to make my own batch and take it to my Wednesday Night Investment Group meeting (read poker buddies). I brought this half-full paper grocery bag full of the stuff to the table. Everybody was intrigued since nobody ever brings food to these "meetings", but I just kind of plopped it down and told them it was popcorn. Their curiosity waned immediately, they all know I love to cook and have all been to my house for at least a dinner or two and I could see the disappointment on their faces. I was disappointed too because I thought at least one of my buddies would at least give it a try. I remember one of my friends, Tim, at least tipped over the edge of the bag and looked inside, but then let it sit without trying it. I started chomping on some thinking the fumes would flame their curiosity but that didn't work either. In desperation I finally announced, "Somebody has to try my popcorn. I made it with bacon."

I got a couple scowls and a mumble or two but still no takers. Finally, "I am not going to play another hand until someone tries my popcorn!" Knowing that sounded a little desperate I thought of an excuse for my whining. "It's a work thing. I need to know if it's any good before I serve it for a special event I'm planning." That finally did the trick and a couple of my friends dug in for a handful. Mission accomplished! Within half an hour the bag was empty and they were all clambering for what I had done.

After the reception we had gotten from guests and friends Chef and I started thinking maybe we were on to something. I thought maybe we needed a little more market research so I made a quadruple batch and took it to my Sunday Night Bocce Ball League (Bocce is kind of like lawn-bowling that, at least here in St. Helena, is more dedicated to eating and drinking amazing things than it is to any kind of competition. In a town of 5,000 about 1,000 people play per week throughout the season). I started passing out tastes. On the third week of passing out little samples one of the players from another team saw me coming and commented, "Here comes Jimmy's Crack Corn. It's so good it's addictive." So, no, for the sake of public safety — and our future profits — Chef and I have decided not to give out our recipe, but if you experiment and your recipe turns out half as good as ours I think you'll be happy.

My wife's family has a celebration meal that has wangled its way into my family's traditions. It is a simple, yet fun and tasty meal that has at its base Fritos Corn Chips. They call it Haystacks. If I had named it I would have called it Tostadas Gone Wild. You start by covering your dinner plate with a layer of Fritos, then a ladle of beans (this can be any number of bean choices, canned pinto beans is the norm, but loose refried beans work well, kidney beans are also a good choice) and then everyone has their own building technique from there, but the choice of ingredients can be huge: iceberg lettuce, mixed greens, chopped green, white or purple onion, sliced olives, crumbled Italian sausage or any other leftover meat or cold cuts you want to slice or dice into bite-sized pieces, shredded or crumbled cheeses, salsa, catsup, salad dressing, sour cream, chopped tomato, cucumber, zucchini, sweet peppers of any color. These are just suggestions that popped into my head, but I think you get the idea. The cool part is that with all the dietary restrictions and preferences that now seem to populate any party, with the exception of the Fritos, the meal can be modified on the fly for almost any propensity.

A couple days after one of these celebratory meals I noticed two bags of the big-scoop Fritos still on the top of my fridge. That would not do, if they stayed in the house they would get opened and devoured. Fritos are "special-occasion" treats that, for so many reasons, can't become everyday snacking food. So I grabbed the two bags as I was heading to work one day and as I entered the Inn I took a hard right into the kitchen. Perfect, Chef Ryan, who had just been with us for a few months at this point was working at the counter, prepping for the Wine Social we do every night. Unceremoniously I chucked the two bags of Fritos onto the counter, turned and walked out of the kitchen. Over my shoulder I declared, "Deal with these!" while continuing into the Front Desk area. I was snickering to myself, but I didn't let Chef see me. Purposefully I avoided him for the next few hours wondering if he was thinking I was just being a complete jerk or if he was taking my cryptic behavior as a food challenge (which is what I was hoping he was thinking).

I couldn't have been more pleased. At our Wine Social that night one of the special appetizers was Frito Crab Melts, a luscious crab salad tucked into a big-scoop Frito topped with melted cheese. Chef strutted these out of the kitchen with his normal swagger but with an additional wry smile like 'Dude, I hit it out of the park MoFo, bring it on!" Certainly I let him know I was impressed and we had a good laugh around the whole thing until I asked, "You used both bags up?"

"No, I still have at least another bag and a quarter," Ryan admitted. I raised my eyebrows and dropped my chin, looking at him over my glasses, "Looks like you have more work to do."

The next night he came out with the most amazingly tasty Southwest Meatballs, using crushed Fritos instead of bread crumbs. We still get a lot of laughs out of this little work episode.

Hot Sweet Bacon
by Ryan

This is one of Chef Ryan's most requested recipes. The description below is more of a technique than a recipe. Keep experimenting until you get your bacon the way you want it. Chef has also used honey and has substituted the chili powder for other spices on the shelf. Recently I made it with some Jamaican Jerk spice my daughter had gotten me of Christmas. It was a little too rock'n for the rest of my family so I had to eat the entire batch over the next few days. Oh well.

INGREDIENTS

½ lb bacon

½ Cup brown sugar,
    approximately

2 tbls chili powder,
    approximately

DIRECTIONS

1. Preheat oven to 425 degrees.

2. Lay bacon out in a single row on a lipped baking sheet. Sprinkle chili powder and then brown sugar over bacon.

3. Bake approximately 12 minutes then flip bacon into the puddle of brown sugar each slice has created. Bake until crispy.

Bacon Wrapped Dates

by Ryan

INGREDIENTS

2 dozen dates, pitted

2 dozen whole Marcona
almonds, roasted

1 small wedge
Cambozola cheese

1 dozen slices high-quality
bacon, cut in half crosswise

DIRECTIONS

1. Preheat oven to 325 degrees.

2. Pit dates if not already pitted. Stuff each date with an almond and a little sliver of cheese.

3. Wrap bacon around date and secure with a toothpick.

4. Place on a cookie sheet and bake until bacon is crispy, about 5 minutes.

Bacon & Spinach Quiche
By Deniese

INGREDIENTS

7 eggs

1/8 cup flour

½ tsp baking powder

1 cup cottage cheese

2 cups jack cheese, shredded

½ cup spinach, drained
and chopped

½ cup bacon, fried crisp
and crumbled

½ tsp salt

½ tsp dried basil (1
tsp if fresh)

1/8 tsp pepper

¼ stick butter

½ onion, chopped

DIRECTIONS

1. Preheat oven to 350 degrees.

2. Melt butter in a skillet and lightly sauté onions, then add spinach and toss together.

3. Combine eggs, flour, baking powder, basil, salt and pepper in separate bowl. Blend well. Stir in all cheeses. Add onion and spinach mixture. Add crumbled bacon and mix.

4. Pour mixture into a greased 9 X 9 greased baking dish. Bake uncovered at 350 degrees for approximately 40 minutes or until golden brown on top. Let stand a few minutes before cutting into squares and serving.

Frito Crab Melts

by Ryan

INGREDIENTS

2 lbs lump crab meat

1 cup mayonnaise

1/3 cup Sriracha Sauce (or other hot sauce)

2 bunches green onions, chopped

Salt and pepper to taste

Fritos Scoops

2 avocado, cut into thumbnail sized pieces

½ lb jack cheese, grated (may need more or less depending on how generous you are with the cheese)

DIRECTIONS

1. Preheat oven to 450 degrees.

2. Mix crab, mayonnaise, Sriracha Sauce, green onion, salt and pepper.

3. Fill each individual Frito scoops with crab mixture and sprinkle with cheese.

4. Bake for about 5 minutes or until cheese begins to melt.

5. Top with avocado pieces and serve immediately.

Chef says if you still have crab mixture grab some fresh bread crumbs and an egg or two and make some crab cakes!

Southwest Meatballs

by Ryan

INGREDIENTS

5 lbs ground beef

3 small cans green
    chilies, diced

½ lb cotija cheese, crumbled

1 bunch cilantro, chopped

1 onion, finely chopped

10 cloves garlic, minced

½ cup tomato paste

1 10oz bag Fritos, crushed

5 eggs

½ tsp black pepper

1 tbls cayenne pepper

2 tbls ground cumin

2 tbls chili powder

DIRECTIONS

1. Preheat oven to 325 degrees.

2. Mix all ingredients by hand and form into golf ball sized portions.

3. Bake on a lipped cookie sheet for 20 minutes or until cooked through. Serve with your favorite BBQ sauce.

CHAPTER 17

The Next 40?

If you had asked me 40 years ago if I thought I would stay in the same job for my entire professional career, and then if I would do all those 40 years in the same location, I would have thought the question was crazy. Back then the Inn was nice and all but the world was so huge and the possibilities so endless. Little did I know how much the Inn would feed me. I am now 62 years old and though there are a million other things I still want to do in my life there are also a few thousand days I would still like to spend at the Inn. New folks are always becoming new friends and treasured return guests, I continue to hire new and interesting staff who eventually become

friends and WOW, there is still so much that can be done with the place.

So what would the next 40 years look like? It is not inconceivable that I could live that long. I would love it if one big piece of the future included my kids. Kelly is with me now and doing a spectacular job, Mike is in the biz and could possibly return to his roots and Alura says she wants to be a chef when she grows up, so who knows? One, two or maybe all of them? Don't tell me it's not possible.

Maybe, just maybe, I can have it all. For years I have had this vision of sitting in the Common Room after breakfast, a little workstation set up, my computer clicking away, only to be interrupted by a return guest strolling over to say hello or a staffer giving me a friendly wave as I stare off trying to think of the perfect word that would complete the next sentence in the third book of the science fiction trilogy I am working on. The first book in the trilogy, *As Worlds Burn* by James Dwight (my pen name), is already published and I am about halfway done with the second installment. So, yeah, if one or two of my kids were running the place I could see where I'd have time to write. Then, if I had that much time maybe I wouldn't be missed too much if my wife and I vaulted off to Christchurch, New Zealand (still on my bucket list) on the spur of the moment or if I vanished for a week or two as I vegged in my backyard chilling and grilling. I could always say I was working on new recipes for the Inn.

But would I even recognize the place in 40 years? Kelly is already chomping at the bit to redo more rooms. I'm sure she would like a little more latitude and a larger budget than I have given her so far to put her stamp on the place. She says she would really like to bust into the bathrooms in the Main Building and update the color schemes and furnishings in some (if not all) of the rooms. She's already given me drawings of what the bathrooms could look like and I fully embrace her ideas. Who wouldn't want a steam-shower, tile floors and a bigger granite vanity? And though I feel like I kicked Gramma out of the rooms a few years back, now I'm the Grandpa she might need to kick out. A small spa and workout room down by the pool? How could that hurt? And then there's the enhanced shaded and cooled outdoor seating I have always wanted on the lower patio. And the lawn redone to include a Bocce Ball court for flinging a few balls in the evening with a plate of simple appetizers from the evening chef we now have on duty (Alura, at 13, already loves making pizza dough from scratch). Whatever "comfort" means for the next generations could certainly be added.

It seems that the more "conveniences" we acquire the less convenient our lives become. Will it be possible to keep the flavor and the comfort of the Inn in the brave new years to come? I hate the new hotel rooms in Vegas that are so completely automated, you step into the room and the curtains open, the lights come on and the music starts. It is a little exciting for a first impression, but when you have to read an instruction manual on how to get the curtains to close or how to have the light stay on if you are sitting quietly reading for half an hour the novelty wears off pretty quickly. So that kind of stuff is out as far as I am concerned. Even TVs? They will likely be passé in a few short years so those are still not in my (or my daughter's) contemplations. A full-blown sit-down restaurant? Na. There are a dozen amazing places we will drive you to and I can't see that changing anytime soon. Solar, of course. A million more bites of download speed, probably. Other little tweaks for the new gadgets or SciFi transportation, sure, but is the need for human connection going to change all that much? Is the desire to slow the f down going to change? I say places like the Inn will be needed all the more. So, epoch changes? I just don't see the need unless folks just don't want to pay the freight for what we offer, but that hasn't happened.

Regardless of the future, I have a lot of people to thank and acknowledge for the amazing life I have enjoyed so far. I certainly couldn't have crafted this wonderful life by myself. The credit for the vast majority of my gratifying life belongs to my wife Lorinda. The incredible luck of finding this woman and roping her into my life at 42 years old was life changing to say the least. Having three amazing children who have navigated their own paths into lives of meaning and comfort deserve a moment of pause and a sincere thank you, as well as a sigh of relief. They are all turning out so beautifully. To my parents I owe a huge thank you for providing me the canvass for me to scribble, erase and color my life's story on. The layers of charcoal, oils and acrylics have jumbled together, overlapped and obscured each other and though I claim no skill in the crafting of that canvass I have to say I am ultimately quite pleased with the results.

To my staff over the years, I owe you so much. Though I have been wildly inappropriate at times, totally lacking in subtlety or grace at others, I have always attempted to be open, honest and caring with all of them. I hope that most of them can see that in me and can accept my thanks as sincere and heart-felt. Without my spectacular staff none of my visions could have been realized.

To all the professionals around me who have either helped guide me or have taken some of the load (or both) I say thank you. Friendships here can be rare, with getting the job done the highest priority, but if one makes laughter at least second on the list any job can become so much more pleasant.

To my partners who have supported and guided me, but for the most part have left me alone, I give a huge shout-out.

Having confidence in me when their money is on the line, that means a lot.

My most sincere and heartfelt thank-yous go out to my guests. Without you absolutely none of this would have been possible. You have made your choices and paid your money and supported me in this most perfect of lives: difficult, challenging, frustrating and at times heartbreaking but more than equally brilliantly uplifting, meaningful, fulfilling, joyous and ultimately spectacular.

Thank you all!

Hot Artichoke Dip

by Judi

This is an example of the collaborative effort the Inn has always been. When we first started offering our wine tastings in the afternoon we had no idea they were going to evolve into one of the key comfort features of the Inn. Those first few tastings were just that, a winery showing up with some wine and we would throw out a couple chunks of cheese and some crackers. Then Deniese jumped into the kitchen one time to throw together a simple appetizer. Wineries were anxious to pour, guests were more than willing to taste the wine and a whole lot of the staff loved to cook, so off it went until we found ourselves serving an elaborate spread every night and almost accidentally finding another piece of now constitutes the soul of the Inn. This simple recipe soon was brought to us by one of our staff and has been a much loved dish for about fifteen years now.

INGREDIENTS

1 cup mayonnaise

1 cup parmesan
        cheese, grated

1 cup cheddar cheese, grated

1 small can Ortega chilies,
        or 4 freshly roasted
        Anaheim chilies

2 roasted jalapenos (optional)

2 cups canned artichokes,
        packed in water,
        drained & chopped

Salt and pepper to taste

DIRECTIONS

1. Preheat oven to 350 degrees.

2. Mix all ingredients in a bowl and pour into an oven-proof serving dish. Bake for 25 minutes or until browned on top. Let stand for ten minutes and garnish with a slice of lemon and a couples sprigs of parsley.

Now, you know if I am going to make this I am going to throw in a large dollop of my roasted garlic or my caramelized onion pates, or one of each. Maybe a teaspoon of balsamic? Let me know.

Lamb Lollipops
by Jim

Gotta be done on the BBQ. And while you have the BBQ heated up think about the recipe above. Brush some excellent bread with garlic olive oil and grill it just before you put the chops on. Then while the chops are cooking cut the hot bread into squares and top with some easily melting or soft cheese that is going to ooze down into the bread a little. Arrange on a serving platter so that there is room in between to squares of bread for the lamb chops as they come off the grill. Believe me, the lamb will be ready before the bread cools.

INGREDIENTS

2 racks of lamb chops

½ cup extra virgin olive oil

8 cloves garlic

½ tsp Dejon mustard (optional)

Salt to taste (a couple good shakes)

More hand-crushed black pepper than you think appropriate

2 sprigs fresh rosemary

DIRECTIONS

1. Take a palmful of black pepper corns and crush them roughly between your cutting board and the bottom of a heavy skillet.

2. Combine all ingredients except the lamb (I like to do this the day before if I think about it). Cut lamb into individual chops and marinate lamb for at least a couple hours in the refrigerator.

3. Remove from refrigerator at least an hour before grilling. Remove lamb from marinade and pat as dry as possible, pushing peppercorns into the meat when possible.

4. Grill over the hottest fire you've got in your backyard until sizzling dark brown on the first side and then how-ever brown you can get them on the second side without cooking them past your desired doneness (I prefer rare to medium rare).

Flare-ups are inevitable with this recipe. A super-hot fire and dripping lamb fat are going to give you flames. I just kind of deal with it, moving the meat around to keep out of the worst flames. I guess you can have a squirt bottle ready and douse the flames as you go but I always seem to forget.

As an appetizer serve these immediately off the grill with no utensils, no sauce or anything except squares of bread grilled sourdough bread (brush a little olive oil on thick slices of sourdough and grill them along with the lamb). Just grab the bone and rip into the meat like a savage (we have a vacant lot behind our fence at home so our guests get an amazing guilty pleasure by chucking the denuded bones over our fence). The bread will sop up the amazing juices so I like to eat the bread last.

While you've got the grill hot here is another favorite that was brought to me by a friend at one of my wife and my epic summer parties we call Chill & Grills. This is an adaptation on the classic pot luck only they are all set up for outside living. Everyone brings something to throw on the BBQ, or a side dish and/or some serious libations. I usually fill one of those spout-jugs full of my secret margarita mix and being in the wine country we usually end up with more bottles of amazing reds than we can drink though since these parties are in the summer the white wines that show up are usually long gone before it has cooled off enough for the reds.

BBQ Yukon Gold Potatoes

By David (a buddy)

INGREDIENTS

8 Medium-sized white potatoes

2 onions, sliced (if you can get your onions about the diameter as the potatoes that is ideal)

3 red, yellow and/or orange sweet bell peppers, cut into squares about the size of the diameter of the potatoes

1 stick butter, melted

Repeated shakes of garlic salt

Salt and pepper to taste

8 6" sheets of aluminum foil

Yukon Golds garnished with chopped green onion

DIRECTIONS

1. Wash and slice each potato into 6 slices, keeping potatoes separate and intact.

2. One at a time place a potato on a sheet of foil. Between each slice place either a slice of onion or a square of sweet pepper and a shake of garlic salt.

3. Form the potato back into a torpedo, forming the foil around it to hold it together. This takes a little practice and patience since each slice of each ingredient seems to want to go its own way.

4. Once you have everything pretty much corralled in the cupped foil pour some of the butter across the slices then salt and pepper to taste.

5. Finish by keeping the sides of the foil tucked in as you roll the potato up like you're rolling a burrito.

6. I use my Big Green Egg to bake them, but they do just fine on the cooler side of a BBQ if you put them on and drop the cover for about 20 minutes before you start cooking your meats. Total baking time is about 40 minutes. I don't turn them so when you open the foil the bottom of the potatoes are nicely browned and the rest is steaming and creamy.

Contents